A TREASURY OF
AMERICAN GARDENING

A TREASURY OF AMERICAN GARDENING

Edited by John R. Whiting

WITH CONTRIBUTIONS BY
T. H. Everett, R. Milton Carleton, Montague Free,
Marjorie P. Johnson, P. P. Pirone, F. F. Rockwell,
Robert S. Lemmon, Helen S. Hull

PHOTOGRAPHS AND ILLUSTRATIONS FROM
Gottscho-Schleisner, Roche, Allianora Rosse, Max Tatch,
Colonial Williamsburg, Richard Averill Smith,
National Council of State Garden Clubs,
The Garden Club of America

FLOWER GROWER—THE HOME GARDEN MAGAZINE
and DOUBLEDAY AND COMPANY, GARDEN CITY, N.Y.

CONTENTS

I

THE GARDEN WRITERS

by John R. Whiting

THE
Compleat Gard'ner;
OR,
Directions for CULTIVATING
AND
Right ORDERING
OF
Fruit-GARDENS
AND
Kitchen-Gardens;
With Divers REFLECTIONS
On several Parts
OF
HUSBANDRY.

In Six BOOKS.

By the Famous Mon^{sr.} *De La Quintinye*,
Chief director of all the GARDENS of the *French*-King.

To which is added
His Treatise of *ORANGE-TREES*, with
the Raising of *MELONS*, omitted in the
French Editions.

Made English by *John Evelyn* Esquire,
Illustrated with Copper Plates.

LONDON,

Printed for *Matthew Gillyflower*, at the *Spread Eagle* in
Westminster-Hall, and *James Partridge*, at the *Post-
house* at *Charing-Cross*, M DC XC III.

UPON the American social scene many changes have come during the mid-century period. Let us skip past the headlined ones-of automobile and paved road, or radio-television, or some college education in nearly half the families. Let us not stop to inquire into the changes in people and their lives because of the new medicine or labor unions. With much less fanfare an ancient occupation has become an avocation of millions. The love of trees, wild flowers, and the husbandry of vegetables and flowers—seemingly a never-changing sort of interest—has been swept up in the technological marvels as rapidly moving as the announcements of new antibiotics, so rapidly that many people otherwise well informed have not yet noticed that home gardening and all its related skills have gone through a great revolution. In this book, I believe, you will be able to take a new kind of look at something that has been happening in suburbs and along R.F.D. routes and even on city roof tops. It is quite a technical revolution, with its plants invented by man, its miracle chemicals, and its vast technological production; but much more, it is a revolution in what *people* do.

The home gardener is part scientist, part artist, part philosopher, part plowman. He modifies the climate around his home. He participates in civic enterprises, exchanges information around the world, and uses poetry and sweat to soothe his troubled self. In *A Treasury of American Gardening*, I believe,

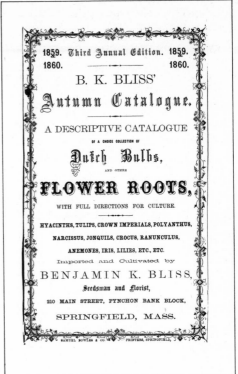

you will find a fresh look at what he has wrought. This book, perhaps, will open your eyes to the greater outdoor beauty that is part of the heritage of the American people.

Not the least of the factors that have been spreading the interest in gardening for a hundred fifty years has been a special type of scientific writer, poet, and instructor—the garden writer. Thomas Jefferson was one. Benjamin Franklin, with his interest and correspondence with scientists, was another. Just as the early books were how-to books, so the next phase, in the second half of the nineteenth century, was one of scholarly contributions to knowledge, for knowledge was increasing as experimental work in the new agricultural experiment stations gave, not only improved plants and trees, but also scientific knowledge of the best ways to garden and operate orchards. But the simpler how-to books, and the many kinds of horticultural magazines, reached still more people.

Seed and nursery catalogues were a part of the average person's garden literature. Indeed one seedsman, Peter Henderson, wrote one of the influential books of the century: *Gardening for Profit,* which with its 150,000 copies helped induce many persons to take up vegetable farming. How much does the American diet of vegetables of every kind owe to the seedsmen who sent their catalogues and instruction books to small rural homes?

Color printing, with human-interest art work that suited its sentimental age just as the drawings of fruits, flowers, and vegetables represented realities, made the seed and nursery catalogue a natural ornament on the dining-room table in the days when winter evenings were still lighted by kerosene lamps. Other men of the seed business who wrote parts of the literature of the art included Joseph Breck, who founded a large firm as well as editing books and magazines on horticulture, and Alfred Conard, who made selling roses by mail his special interest. This was soon after the Civil War, when Conard found he could propagate good roses faster than he could sell them at wholesale. Today's Conard-Pyle is the descendant.

One of the catalogue covers shown with this chapter is that of W. Atlee Burpee, whose name was known to every home gardener and many a city dweller even in 1894. By advertising in innumerable newspapers and magazines the Burpee Company built a special kind of friendship with small home-owners as well as large-scale farmers who wanted to grow vegetables and flowers.

In Chicago, Vaughan's Seed Company was another that helped to spread information on gardening as well as the seeds and equipment that the amateur tiller needed. Similarly Jackson and Perkins grew from a giant wholesaler of roses to be also a giant of mail-order retailing.

The seed and nursery companies, indeed, are only following in the tradition of such famous names as that of William Prince, who established a nursery and issued a catalogue at Flushing, New York, before the middle of the eighteenth century. One of the succeeding Princes, a century later, introduced the Lombardy poplar into the American nursery trade. The two Prince gardens, one called the Old American Nursery and the other called the Linnean Botanic Garden, were great show places of horticulture, and their catalogues, in turn, were among the standard horticultural publications of their time. Another Flushing nursery, that of Samuel Parsons, was the first to introduce Japanese maples and the first to propagate rhododendrons. Mr. Parsons, as a landscape gardener, influenced garden design and, as a writer, brought information on gardening to many hobbyists.

Perhaps no one would dispute that at the top of Grand Old Masters of horticultural writers has been the name of Liberty Hyde Bailey. Last year, when the American Horticultural Council sent him a congratulatory message on his ninety-sixth birthday, he listened to it with interest and acknowledged appropriately. To a knowing home gardener the name of Bailey has been one of the most memorable. He taught, experimented, traveled, wrote twoscore

11

JUNE, 1872.

AMERICAN

AGRICULTURIST,

FOR THE FARM, GARDEN & HOUSEHOLD.

Vol. XXXI. Number 6.

PUBLISHED BY

ORANGE JUDD & CO.,

245 BROADWAY,

NEW YORK.

books, edited or contributed to many of the finest agricultural and horticultural publications of the nineteenth century. Both Michigan State and Cornell owe part of their greatness to Bailey's sojourns there. His *Annals of Horticul-*

12

ture, for the years 1890 through 1894, was in some ways the indirect idea for the book you hold in your hand. Bailey once wrote:

> An important feature of American horticulture is its living literature. Persons may care nothing for books; yet the literature of any subject is the measure of its ideals. . . . There is no reason for literature if it does not inspire and point to better things. We measure the aspirations of any time by its writings. Whether the fact be recognized or not, the literature of our horticulture is an underlying force which slowly dominates the thoughts and ideals of men.

But this is not an exclusive preserve for the great and famous. Walk through your garden on a pre-spring day, make a list of the buds and early flowers, and you are a garden reporter. Go for a woodland walk, come back and tell the story of the wild flowers you saw, and you are a garden writer.

Today garden writing is in another stage of rebirth, as it, like other special writing, must go through a change with each new period. The professional editor, with his demands for clarity and sharp focus, may well change the profession of horticultural writing as he has changed medical and other scientific writing. The millions of new readers, with their interest in visual methods of presentation, have brought the photograph, the chart, and the step-by-step drawing to a new importance in books and magazines. Garden books sell more copies than were dreamed of in former decades. Newspaper garden sections outprosper those of sports and movies. Many magazines that appeal to the home garden enthusiast are, for the first time in America, reaching for well over half a million circulation. This past year *Horticulture,* the oldest, celebrated its fiftieth year as the official publication of the Massachusetts Horticultural Society and *Flower Grower, The Home Garden Magazine,* its fortieth year. Meanwhile many of the plant societies and other horticultural organizations published quarterly, annual, and monthly magazines, and often beautiful, instructive books. Photographers and artists, who communicate with pictures, are a part of this complex activity; they are the most graphic of all the garden "writers."

The Garden Writers Association, true to the mail-order custom of many home gardeners, began to grow as a kind of "mail-order professional organization," issuing a now-and-then bulletin by mail, and holding its annual meeting in conjunction with the American Horticultural Council. Nearly two hundred newspaper, radio, TV, magazine, and other kinds of specialists now belong.

Some American gardeners began to discover that one of the interesting bypaths of gardening is the collecting of early books on the subject. A gardener with a taste for history, looking at a copy of Bernard M'Mahon's *American Gardener's Calendar,* can note that M'Mahon introduced the plants collected by

Horticulture, at first a weekly, and *Flower Grower,* at first for gladiolus specialists, began publication in the early part of the century.

Lewis and Clark on their expedition and presented the first landscaping suggestions to American gardeners. One book-loving man, C. W. Wood, of Copemish, Michigan, has made his hobby of collecting gardening first editions into a mail-order business that he runs from a beautiful part of the northern peninsula. Others collect old catalogues or old floral prints. An avocation like gardening can have many other hobbies interwoven into its fabric—photographing flowers in color, building stone terraces, arranging flowers in antique containers, or traveling to famous gardens.

In the pages of this book you will see over many garden walls, walk down many garden paths, and discover, perhaps, why early morning is a special time for gardeners, why stones, rustling leaves, and Latin names of flowers are all parts of a great human adventure: gardening.

II

ALL THE HOME GARDENERS

by T. H. Everett

PHOTOGRAPHY BY ROCHE

Today's home gardeners especially like these smaller-flowered pompon-type dahlias, but members of the American Dahlia Society can specialize in many other types. A few of the classes that are dear to the dahlia hobbyist are formal and informal decorative, collarette, single, miniature and cactus-flowered.

O VER thirty million gardeners in the United States. That is the number given by reliable estimators; that is the figure that *The Saturday Evening Post* mentioned in an article in 1953. Gardening is one of America's most popular hobbies. What primal urges motivate its followers? Just why do people "dig in the dirt"?

Ask a dozen green-thumbers and would-be green-thumbers this question and you are likely to get as many different answers. There is no *one* reason why people garden, although most gardeners would agree, in the idiom of the day, that they do it for fun.

By fun they mean the satisfying of some deep-seated desire and, less consciously, the opportunity to escape, even temporarily, from the stresses of modern life.

The urge to create gardens and to grow things is undoubtedly stronger in some people than in others. I am quite sure that in any large population there exist those who abhor all thoughts of tending plants and neither want to garden nor would be happy gardening. To admit this is not popular among the dedicated—and why should it be? What swain accepts the fact that his loved one is less attractive to others than to himself?

Let us not waste time or shed tears on the unrepentant few who have

There are more than 13,000 members of the American Rose Society—members who like to be known as rosarians. They and thousands of other gardeners cultivate the rose—climbers, ramblers, shrub forms, hybrid teas, hybrid perpetuals, floribundas, and a recent addition, the grandiflora.

really tried gardening and found it not to their liking. Their satisfactions must be sought elsewhere. They can no more know the joys of growing flowers and fruits and lawns and vegetables and trees and shrubs and evergreens than a color-blind person can thrill to a sunset or a tone-deaf person can appreciate a symphony.

Let us consider rather those who like to garden, or who would like to if given the opportunity; let us reserve our proselyting and missionary work for those we may reasonably hope to convert, the people who have never gardened, and those who have done a little but have as yet only a lukewarm attachment to the soil.

Probably most people begin gardening with a specific, practical purpose in mind. The most common objective is to "fix up the yard," to add to the appearance and value of the house; thus new homeowners and house occupiers are the group most susceptible to being bitten by the gardening bug. They are naturals, push-overs for ideas concerning verdant lawns, shade trees, evergreens, and flowers. Other beginners harbor vague thoughts that it would be nice to produce their vegetables or fruit, and scarce a woman there is who at the mere mention of a garden does not envisage quantities of flowers—flowers

One of the oldest garden flowers with a turbulent history is the object of one of our newest plant societies, the National Tulip Society, incorporated in 1947. Tulipomania was the craze that began in 1634 in Holland. Fabulous prices were paid for a single bulb, crowds rioted, and a royal decree was required to quiet the speculators.

to be cut and hauled indoors to display in vases and to play their parts in arrangements—perhaps even to be exhibited triumphantly before the local garden club.

These are practical, and justifiable, reasons for taking up the spading fork and hoe, for tending the sprinkler, and wielding the spray gun. Such efforts are means to ends and at first, at least, it is the end that is all-important. With the realization or part realization of this objective a tremendous satisfaction results. Gardening is a creative art and the new gardener rightly feels a deep pride of accomplishment as he sees his plot develop and become more lovely as the result of his planting and care as he gradually molds it to complement his house—to express his personality. Not less intense is the contentment that results from serving home-grown vegetables at table or from having a plenitude of home-produced herbs for the housewife to use cunningly. The joy of being able to cut flowers freely, lavishly, to decorate the house and to give to friends is an end that justifies a lot of gardening effort . . . and so, I am told, does the winning of a blue ribbon for a flower arrangement made possible by the use of unusual blooms grown at home.

These are obvious reasons for gardening, examples of end results that

Members of the American Iris Society may specialize in the bearded, or German, iris, but they also include in their gardens Japanese iris, Siberian, and
various bulbous-rooted kinds.

provide logic for effort and cash expended—purposes that the beginner most
usually claims as his motivations—and they often are practical achievements
that all may see and comprehend. But many people have deeper and more
compelling reasons to till the soil; for many the end results are not the greatest joy. Gardening for them is not only a means; it is an end in itself. They
know the tremendous satisfaction that is to be had from tilling the earth, from
nursing plants from youth to maturity and from sickness to vigor, from propagating new plants, from creating pictures with living vegetation. Gardening
brings its devotee close to nature; it reveals both achievements and limita-
tions that man has made and met in his progress towards mastery of the green
resources of the earth. Gardening is soul-satisfying to many.

Frequently the man, or woman, who begins to garden with a specific,
practical objective in view finds that the greatest joy comes from the doing
rather than from the accomplishment, and a new convert is made.

Let me try to present to you some of the pleasures that are to be had
from gardening, some of the satisfactions that thirty million Americans enjoy
in whole or part. First there is the joy to be had from doing the immediate
job at hand. It may be a simple repetitive task like weeding a lawn or spad-

LILY Sunburst

The North American Lily Society leads in present-day worship of the lily. The ever-lovely Madonna and regal lilies must now vie with many hybrids, some similar to the Aurelian lily Sunburst with reflexed petals, others with cup-shaped flowers in rainbow colors.

ing a piece of ground in readiness for planting . . . seemingly irksome chores perhaps to the uninitiated but labors of love to the true gardener. As a mother finds pleasure in attending to tasks that promote the welfare of her offspring, so the ardent cultivator finds joy in engaging in work that furthers the well-being of his plants. To take a spade or spading fork on a crisp fall day and without undue haste or backbreaking effort to turn over slice after slice of sweet-smelling brown earth can bring rich pleasure to the gardener who fully understands just what he is accomplishing. He knows that the manure, compost, and even weeds he is burying will be gradually changed in the laboratory of the soil into black amorphous humus that will improve the quality of his earth and gradually yield its store of nutrients to next year's crops. He knows too that with each twist of the spade he is bringing to the surface fresh portions of soil to be acted upon favorably by the winter elements, that by loosening the mold he is improving its drainage and promoting the growth of those favorable soil microorganisms with which every fertile soil is teeming. He is making ready for spring, he is looking forward to another season, he is preparing for the future . . . and that is what keeps gardeners young in spirit.

Pruning is a highly agreeable task to the gardener who knows his job,

24

Not all peonies bear globular, many-petaled flowers.
The variety shown here is an anemone-flowered
type, one of several recognized by the venerable
American Peony Society, which was incorporated
in 1904.

to the one who can approach a tangled, overgrown shrub border, a tall and
leggy lilac, or a long-neglected climbing rose with assurance and with full
control over himself and his pruning tools. As each considered cut is made he
sees improvement and promise in those branches he allows to remain for the
future. How less onerous is his task than that of the person who has not learned
the art of pruning, who butchers his trees and shrubs unmercifully, or neglects
them entirely . . . and how much surer his reward.

I mentioned weeding a lawn—a tiresome task you say—and yet I have
spent many happy hours on pleasant summer days, a dinner knife with sawed-
off blade in hand, uprooting pesky weeds. One can get a considerable area
cleaned on a lazy summer afternoon and there is satisfaction in that, but the
greater satisfaction comes from the contemplative opportunities the task
affords—it gives one time to think—and as one grubs out chickweed, dande-
lion, and stripling crab grass the mind ranges widely over a variety of problems and subjects, and, being close to the earth, difficulties seem to be the
easier resolved. I do not advocate hand weeding as the only means of eradi-
cating intruders in the sward; modern science has given us many helpful
chemical aids for doing that, but even science has not, I think, given us an

Sweet Cicely is the popular name for *Myrrhis odorata,* a perennial herb with anise-flavored roots, seeds, and leaves. Members of the Herb Society of America can supply much lore on this plant as well as on others high in aroma, flavor, or medicinal properties.

adequate substitute for the pleasant exercise of hand weeding—and of thinking the while—on a day when it is a joy to be out in the sunshine and air with a good excuse for taking life easily. Certainly television is not the answer.

The true gardener enjoys—really enjoys—the doing of all manner of tasks concerned with his hobby. Provided he understands the reasons for what he is doing and is familiar with the results he may expect, his pleasure is assured. Such unrelated and widely divergent jobs as washing flowerpots, sowing seeds, pinching chrysanthemums, probing for borers, and spreading fertilizer, as well as many others, are immediate satisfactions.

But the joy of working in a garden, and the healthful exercise it implies, the contentment that results from doing well a task that needs doing are passing pleasures that end with the job. More lasting contentments arise from long-term accomplishments, from specializing in one or more phases of the hobby and in learning about plants and the environments in which they grow. Nor must we overlook the pleasure that is to be had from meeting fellow gardeners, at clubs, societies, shows, and over the garden fence, as well as getting to know almost as intimately those who write on the subject in the pages of magazines and books. Let us consider some further phases of gardening.

Rhododendrons, the deciduous species of which are usually called azaleas, are valued for their handsome evergreen foliage and for their magnificent flowers. Gardeners who favor them are invited to belong to the American Rhododendron Society.

Vegetable growing often makes a particular appeal to men. It is a grand speciality, for here as nowhere else, unless it be fruit growing, the beginner is able to judge the quality of his results, and, even though pride of achievement blind him to realities, his family is usually quick to point out any deficiencies.

The growing of a kitchen garden means better eating, for aside from the fact that crops may be harvested before they become too old and eaten before they have staled in transit or market place, the home vegetable gardener benefits because he can select the finest table varieties, kinds that are rarely grown commercially because heavy cropping, appearance, uniformity, and ability to travel well are of necessity considered more important than mere flavor by the market grower. Whoever has savored a first mess of June peas cooked fresh from the garden or who knows the flavor and tenderness of corn picked at just the right stage and consigned to the pot within ten minutes of being taken from the stalk needs no selling on the advantages of growing one's own, and a well-stocked deep freeze may serve through the winter as a happy reminder of gardening days past . . . and of others to come.

The vegetable gardener's crops are mostly annuals and so each year he

It is easy to see why fuchsia has been known as lady's-eardrop. This tender shrub is very popular with gardeners on the West Coast, where the American Fuchsia Society was founded.

knows the joy of making a new beginning, and each year, if he works wisely, he sees his soil improve and mellow and become easier to work and more responsive. No other gardening effort invests its followers with a better understanding of the soil than does the growing of a vegetable patch.

The attractions of fruit growing, aside from the fact that edible crops are the end purpose, are quite different from those of cultivating vegetables and appeal to rather different temperaments. Many, many more people *think* they are going to enjoy fruit growing than actually do. These are often uninformed beginners naïve enough to visualize a work-free or nearly work-free garden, and plants of delicious produce. Nothing could be further from the truth; to grow good fruit requires timely attention, as does all gardening. The successful raiser of fruits must be patient at first; normally he must wait longer, sometimes much longer, for returns from his labor than the cultivator of onions and carrots, peas and tomatoes. The individual plants he cares for will be fewer, but each, at least in the case of the tree fruits, assumes a distinct personality and must be treated according to its needs. One variety of apple requires pruning differently from another; an apple grafted on dwarfing stock requires care distinct from one on seedling stock; red raspberries

Trees, whether they grow in front or back yard, along boulevards, in forests, or reach magnificent maturity on rolling countryside, are in the province of all gardeners. Particularly are they the concern of members of the American Forestry Association and the National Shade Tree Conference.

and black raspberries are not treated identically, nor are sweet and sour cherries. The fruit grower is a long-term investor and needs to be knowledgeable about the trees, bushes, and vines he tends. Perhaps more than most home gardeners the cultivator of fruits learns to rely upon the advice and help of his State Agricultural Experimental Station and to seek the friendship of the county agent. Although amateur fruit growers are fewer in number than amateur vegetable gardeners, they get no less satisfaction from their hobby. From the homeowner in the subtropics, proud of his orange tree or mango, to the son of Italy who tends a solitary fig tree in a New York back yard, carefully wrapping it each fall in blankets, burlap, or roofing paper to protect it from wintry blasts, there are many, many different kinds of amateur fruit growers; they are people who gain satisfaction from their hobby in fairly direct proportion to what they know about it; fruit growing appeals most to the gardener who likes to keep informed and is willing to go to some small trouble to do so, because only in this way is the success of fruit growing assured.

A good lawn is conceded by all who garden to be a wonderful asset, and most gardeners suffer minor setbacks in pursuit of the ideal. Some fall

English holly (*Ilex aquifolium*) is so well established in the Pacific Northwest that quantities of red-berried sprays are cut each Christmas as a commercial project. Of interest to gardeners is the fact that English holly will grow from Cape Cod to Georgia. Members of the American Holly Society are working to extend the range of this species as well as of the American holly (*Ilex opaca*).

by the wayside and settle for swards far less than good, while others attain a fairly high standard without too much enthusiasm for the work involved; they would prefer to devote the time and money they spend on grass to their roses or vegetables or flower beds, but a minority make the attainment of the perfect lawn their foremost goal and in satisfying this desire enjoy pleasures the equal of those afforded by any other gardening activity. I have known many such gardeners. All are meticulous people, their borders precisely planted, their hedges trimly clipped, their beds neatly mulched; there is an orderliness about their gardens, and usually about their homes and persons. To the lawn perfectionist a single weed is anathema, an untrimmed verge a cause for worry. Such people derive sensuous gratification from merely strolling over rich, thick grass. They survey the results of their handiwork at all seasons with pride and pleasure. A fine lawn *is* a concrete achievement; its attainment calls for wise preparation of the soil before sowing and careful upkeep—fertilizing, watering, weeding, mowing, and disease and pest control through the years—and yet not much more time or effort is needed to have a good lawn than a mediocre one; it is just a matter of dedicating oneself to the proposition that a perfect lawn is attainable, gaining the know-how and

There are begonias that are prized for their foliage, and others, such as the tuberous begonia, that have beautiful flowers. All are of interest to house-plant enthusiasts, lath-house gardeners and people who garden in the shade. *The Begonian* is a monthly publication of the American Begonia Society.

applying oneself to the task. And some gardeners do this with astonishing dividends in results and pleasure.

Amateur growers of flowers are a varied group. They garden for a multitude of reasons and reap diverse enjoyments. They include those whose attitude closely parallels that of the vegetable gardener who likes to grow many varieties, who seeks high-quality produce, and whose avowed purpose is to put the products of his labor to practical use, in the case of the flower hobbyist to decorate the garden or the home. Such individuals lean heavily toward showy flowers and improved horticultural varieties; they are less impressed by rare species of modest mien that may thrill the rock-garden specialist or spark the enthusiasm of the wild-flower addict, yet they are not likely to pursue avidly the newest and most costly novelties as do the one-flower specialists, the dahlia enthusiasts, the rose experts, and the chrysanthemum worshipers, for example. These amateur growers of a general line are a well-balanced lot, varied in their knowledge and experience and likely to value highly the relaxation and quiet enjoyment their hobby brings. You see them in their thousands at the great flower shows that erupt across the land in spring; you find them at the seed stores and garden marts; they belong to

No member of the American Delphinium Society
will part with yearbooks of the Society, which has
fostered the highly developed horticultural varieties
available for the garden today. The florets of the
spiked blooms are characterized by their large
spurs, and range in color from pinks to blue and
white.

garden clubs and horticultural societies and botanical gardens; they read
horticultural books and magazines, and take courses in gardening. They are
the real backbone of flower gardening; they provide chief support for the
commercial raiser of seeds and plants and distributor of flower-garden supplies; from their ranks arise the amateur specialists.

As flower cosmopolites, they enjoy many advantages. Their gardens
bloom from spring to fall, from the arrival of the first crocus to the departure
of the last chrysanthemum, and they enjoy the whole procession. Favorites
they may have, but they are not rabid enough about the merits of any flower
to devote more than a fair share of time to it. They diversify their interests
and thus spread their risks; a poor zinnia year may mean a good aster year,
a fine crop of delphiniums may offset a poor showing by tulips, and so it
goes. Each day and each week end from spring to fall the grower of a mixed
flower garden finds something interesting to do and some new delight to reward him for his efforts, and when local flower-show time comes around he
can usually find some worthy blooms to enter in the horticultural classes,
although sadly enough he too often fails to do so.

Quite different in his outlook and·in the satisfactions his avocation

This primrose is typical of the hardy species grown in gardens from coast to coast. Others can be seen flowering in greenhouses, especially around Easter. The American Primrose Society was incorporated in 1941.

brings is the one-flower specialist. Here is the individual who really *grows* and *knows* the flowers he has made his own. He cultivates the best; nothing he can do is too much trouble or is too good for his favorites. He is an ardent pursuer of his hobby.

Sometimes the absorbing interest of the one-flower specialist is actually confined to one flower like the rose, the gladiolus, or the peony; in other cases it is limited to a small group of nearly related plants such as gloxinias and their kin; occasionally it finds expression in devotion to varieties of plants that require essentially similar culture. To this last group belong the cactus and succulent fans and the specialists in aquatic plants.

No matter which plant or group of plants he favors the one-flower specialist makes himself the master of his hobby. He is an enthusiast and a perfectionist. His devotion brings him satisfactions of a high order. Satisfactions such as those of the dahlia grower who, while spreading an insulating and nourishing mulch over the roots of his plants in June, sees in his mind's eye flower-show judges at a later date examining with keen approval his finest blooms, blooms that owe some of their magnificence to the very task he performs that day. Secure in his certainty of the good he is doing, he applies

42

A bromeliad is a plant in the pineapple family. Plants in this versatile group, also called air plants, have given exciting new house plants. Vriesia, with colorful foliage and brilliant, long-lasting flowers, is an example. There is a Bromeliad Society.

himself with added zeal, and dreams the while, perhaps, of many blue ribbons.

Or consider the pleasures of the housewife who has installed in her basement batteries of fluorescent lights under which she cultivates as complete a collection of African violets as possible. Within the four walls of her home she has a living, constantly blooming garden. The flowers that are her reward are white and pink and blue and lavender and purple and variegated . . . and single and double, the leaves soft, fuzzy, and heart-shaped, and each, she knows, the potential parent of another plant.

Did I refer to the flowers as this housewife's reward? In part that is true, of course, but her deeper pleasures come from caring for these living plants, which are as dependent upon outside ministrations as is an incubator baby, and so, as she pokes the stalk of a leaf cutting into its vermiculite bed or pots the rooted plant a few weeks later, as she waters and fertilizes and fusses over the charges in her cellar garden, she knows special joys.

Though snow falls or the temperature outside registers a chilly zero a tiny section of Africa is abloom inside . . . and because of her attentions. As she surveys the plants she tends and grows this housewife anticipates with pleasure the happiness that her surplus will bring to friends, both sick and

45

Hybridizing has produced a multitude of color and forms in this fragile-looking flower, which is native to Africa. It is the most popular flowering house plant today, and its enthusiastic collectors belong to the African Violet Society of America.

well, with whom she plans to share them. One African violet can lead to many.

But dahlia growers and cultivators of African violets have no monopoly of the special pleasures that belong to one-flower specialists. Consider, if you will, the anticipatory delights of the chrysanthemum grower who knows so well that the tiny rooted plants he sets out in April at such incredibly great distances apart (or so it seems) will, by fall, be massive specimens well clothed with foliage to the ground and so covered with flowers that scarcely a leaf can be seen. It is then, he muses as he plants his rooted cuttings, that the rose growers, the dahlia fans, the iris specialists, and others will do his flower homage, and properly so, for, he asks himself, are not mums the grandest flowers of all? And in October we are inclined to agree. And so each specialist grows the flowers of his taste and his choice. There is room for all in this great gardening field.

Most often the one-flower specialist belongs to a group or society that has made his favorite its own; occasionally he works without any such attachment. Not infrequently, as a result of broadened associations and passing years, he organizes those of kindred interest to form a new society and thus a step forward is taken in furthering interest in, and understanding of, the flower

The fast rise in popularity of one house plant, the African violet, has focused attention on other close relatives to such an extent that the American Gesneria Society was incorporated in 1952. The episcia, with red, purple, or white flowers, is one of these.

or plant selected for this attention. Special plant societies elect officers, hold meetings, read papers, sponsor lectures, organize shows, publish proceedings, journals, and yearbooks, register new varieties, conduct tests, support plant-seeking expeditions, and in other ways make substantial contributions to the horticultural and botanical status of their chosen objects of study. They are one of the most significant factors in American horticulture, for Americans are by nature joiners and by belonging to such societies they achieve much more of permanent good than they could possibly hope to effect as individuals. In addition they enjoy the satisfaction of belonging to a worth-while organization and the company of like-minded fellows. The herding instinct, strong in all except confirmed hermits, finds another useful outlet.

In the United States there are at least forty societies specializing in particular plants, most of nationwide scope. They include the powerful American Rose Society, with more than thirteen thousand members, and the American Orchid Society and American Camellia Society, each with a membership of more than five thousand. There are societies devoted to the special interests of fanciers of delphiniums, begonias, dahlias, ferns, fuchsias, hibiscus, penstemons, and day lilies, to mention but a few.

Coming from the warm, humid regions of Brazil, the gloxinia looks as exotic as it really is. Protect it from strong sun and its large, curiously marked flowers will last for a long while. Membership in the American Gloxinia Society exceeds three thousand.

One of the most amazing developments of recent years is the growth of groups interested in African violets and their relatives. Here belong the phenomenally mushrooming and convention-minded African Violet Society of America, which, among its other activities, publishes a handsome quarterly magazine, the American Gloxinia Society, which boasts more than three thousand members, and the American Gesneria Society. The fact that thousands of Americans, indeed tens of thousands of men and women, are intensely interested in cultivating and caring for a plant of modest stature and deportment that has its native home close by Africa's Mount Kilimanjaro is surely not without its social significance.

Often with the passing of years the amateur specialist "goes commercial," his avocation becomes his vocation, and other amateurs are then enabled to buy the results of his skill and benefit directly from his hard-won experience. This development is a natural one, for usually long before he turns professional and, even though he resists the temptation to do so, he knows far more about his own favorite flower than do most professional growers and he grows his specimens as well or better. His path just naturally brings him in contact with many professionals, his love for his specialty leads him to grow

This hardy cactus is native in Eastern Canada, through Massachusetts, to Alabama and Missouri, regions not usually considered cactus country. Other opuntias bear edible fruit called prickly pears. These as well as other cacti were the reason for the founding of the Cactus and Succulent Society of America.

far more than he needs for himself, and the professional path is usually the only logical one that permits him to devote his whole time to his hobby; professionalism is at once a reason and a rationalization. Among amateurs who have made outstanding contributions to their hobbies there come to mind one of the country's top photographers, who centered his attentions on delphiniums, a druggist and a lawyer whose major loves are iris, a doctor and a lawyer who grow roses of unsurpassed quality, a minister who devotes the major portion of his spare time to gladioli, a businessman who turned to geraniums . . . and the list could be lengthened almost indefinitely. These one-flower hobbyists make it their business to know all there is to know about their choices. They keep in close touch with scientific work that is done in the special fields in which they are interested and with all latest developments; they know all the newest varieties and in their endeavors to produce the finest they learn the supreme importance of close observation, early diagnosis, and attention to minutest detail. They are the most expert of gardeners in their own particular fields. Two of the greatest satisfactions they achieve come from competing with other experts and from helping lesser fry in their efforts to attain the heights.

DAY LILY Firedance

The large patches of orange day lilies (*Hemerocallis* is the botanical name, from the Greek for "beautiful for a day") growing along highways, country lanes, and in waste places are familiar to gardeners and non-gardeners alike. They are usually referred to as "tiger lilies." These escapes from civilization, together with other species, have given numerous hybrids for our gardens. The Hemerocallis Society is one of the most active of the plant societies.

The gardener who specializes is likely, sooner or later, to be irresistibly attracted to that most creative of horticultural activities, the breeding of new flowers. The urge to attempt the production of varieties new, superior, more beautiful than any previously known is strong and is based on a fundamental human desire to better the best we have; it is part of the compelling, driving force that, persisting through generations, has carried man so far in his struggle upward and forward. Perhaps there is no satisfaction to be had from gardening as great as that of the breeder who gives to the world superior kinds of plants, for it is in these that the result of man's work comes closest to divine achievement.

A great many amateurs, and people who began as such, have had notable success as plant breeders. Horticulture owes a debt of gratitude to them. There is little reason for presenting here a lengthy list of such benefactors, but to name a few may sharpen appreciation of the fact that amateur gardeners make important contributions to the horticultural progress and to the cultural well-being of the nation. A college professor at Clinton, New York, the late Professor A. P. Saunders, as a result of forty years or more of patient labor, produced for American gardens a magnificent series of hybrid

54

An amateur plant breeder is taking pollen from one bearded iris to brush onto another variety in the hope that an outstanding seedling will result. Each year amateur and professional breeders are responsible for many new varieties of roses, chrysanthemums, day lilies, gladioli, tulips, and other plants. Some of them belong to an organization known as the Plant Propagators Society.

peonies. More than a year elapses from the sowing of a peony seed until the first tender sprout appears above ground; several seasons must pass before the new plant blooms. The immensity of the professor's labors is appreciated only if one considers the long list of splendid new varieties he raised; of those Dr. John C. Wister wrote in 1953: "It will take two more decades, however, for them to be evaluated properly, for it will take that much time for the stocks to be increased enough, so that they will be available in quantity, widely distributed and known by the great mass of American gardeners. Only then can the great range of type, form and color, and the long season of bloom, that he has made possible for the peony world, be properly appreciated." Twenty years after his death before the latest of Professor Saunders' peonies are likely to become reasonably plentiful! Gardeners yet unborn may see some of them first become abundant. I knew Dr. Saunders and sensed, I think, a little of the deep satisfaction his work brought him; no less will be the happiness his peonies bring to others for many decades to come.

In Cincinnati, A. E. Curtis, a gardening hobbyist, made breeding oriental poppies his specialty. When the depression came and his business of supplying hard-to-get books and back issues of magazines to college libraries

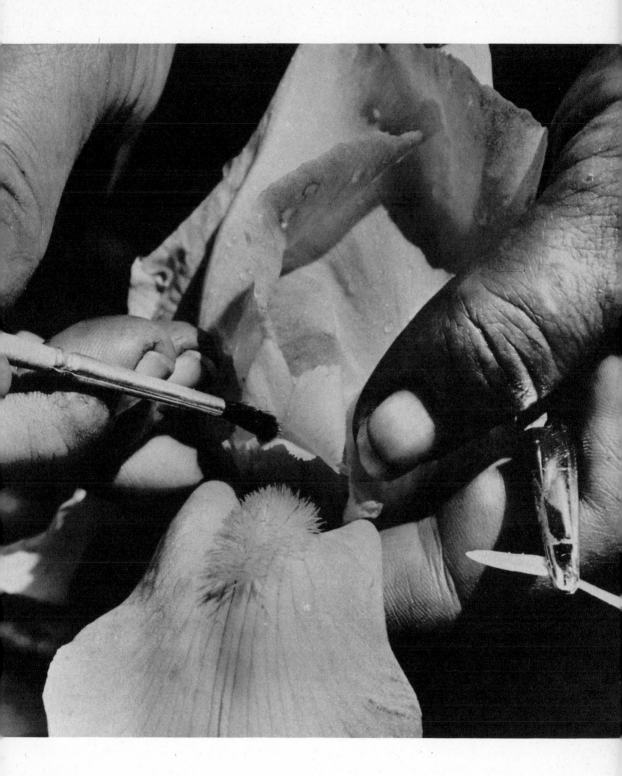

The lemon geranium (*Pelargonium Limoneum*) is one of many aromatic-leaved geraniums. Others include the velvetlike peppermint geranium, nutmeg geranium, and rose geranium. Members of the International Geranium and Pelargonium Society grow these types as well as common but colorful everyday varieties.

vanished, he had to seek, at a time of life when many men are thinking about retirement, a new business. His gardening hobby provided him with that. In his own back yard he found the work and source of income he desired. A. E. Curtis has developed the finest oriental poppies extant. Gardens in America and in other parts of the world have benefited immeasurably from the great work of this quiet Cincinnatian, yet comparatively few outside the ranks of specialists know much about him. This undoubtedly is as he wishes it to be, for A. E. Curtis, like most great plant breeders, is a modest man in love with his work and his flowers. His great satisfaction comes from the work he does rather than from public acclaim.

The breeding of hardier, longer-blooming, disease-resistant roses was the hobby that became the business of a lawyer and his wife at Little Compton, Rhode Island. The Walter D. Brownells, as a result of almost half a century of rose breeding, have produced many splendid varieties, their latest achievements being ever-blooming pillar roses.

Each year, now, with the help of their sons, they raise for trial 20,000 new seedling roses. Most of these are discarded as not being up to the high standards they set; a few are preserved, propagated, and after seven years are

These fronds are carrying spore cases that are part of the fern's reproductive system. The American Fern Society publishes a quarterly journal for its members.

offered for sale. Rose breeding by the Brownells is now a considerable business, yet, as they point out, "the hybridizing at Little Compton, Rhode Island, started with a small rose garden. There was no thought of hybridizing when the first rose garden was planted." And that is about the way many outstanding plant breeders begin.

There are many other men and women amateur gardeners who have had outstanding success in breeding new kinds of plants and who have had plenty of fun doing so. I think of the late Charles Dexter, of Cape Cod, Massachusetts, who gave to us the magnificent Dexter hybrid rhododendrons and azaleas, the late Sam Everett, of Huntington, New York, who also specialized in rhododendrons and azaleas, Kenneth D. Smith, of Staten Island, New York, who has made breeding unusual irises his particular hobby, and Martin R. Jacobus, of Ridgefield, New Jersey, who produced such splendid roses as Dream Girl and Golden Jubilee. Today amateurs across the nation are producing new and better begonias, African violets, camellias, and a host of other plants. Each is engaged in a hobby so intriguing, stimulating, and pregnant with promise that in following it the hobbyist not only finds pleasure and satisfaction, but probably adds to the days of his years as well.

61

This is an important flowering shrub for the South, warm climates of the West Coast area, and Northern greenhouses. Though related to the hardy rose-of-Sharon, the tropical hibiscus is generally more showy. The American Hibiscus Society was incorporated in 1950.

The cultivation of wild flowers makes a very special appeal. It satisfies a natural longing to be close to the things of one's homeland; to know more intimately the factors of one's immediate habitat. An acquaintance with wild flowers, like familiarity with native birds and animals, is part of any worthwhile education. Many Americans extend this phase of their knowledge by growing in their gardens well-loved native plants, by tending and observing them, not only at their seasons of full glory, but throughout the year. To such enthusiasts success with a difficult-to-grow violet or gentian brings as much joy as the establishment of a choice orchid, but lesser kinds bring no less pleasure.

Depending upon the part of the country in which he lives and upon the character of his lot, the cultivator of wild flowers may concentrate largely upon plants of the woodlands or of the plains, of the deserts or of the mountains; there are those who have fun with swamp and bog plants and tame the curious sundews and pitcher plants, the Louisiana iris and the delightful grass of Parnassus. Cacti and other xerophytes are naturals for gardeners who live in warm, dry climes; I know amateurs who specialize in native plants of our seashores. It matters not which group the gardener selects as a specialty, for all

63

Camellias are shrubs for warm climates, but North-
erners can enjoy them in greenhouses. One species,
Camellia sasanqua and its varieties, is hardy enough
for sheltered areas in cold climates. Southerners,
and Californians, are the real camellia hobbyists.
Camellia specialists may join the American Camellia Society.

are intensely interesting; the cultivation of American wildings gives a generous
measure of satisfaction to all who make them their hobby.

I recall a day spent some years ago with the owner of a vast estate.
His domain extended well over a thousand acres; his gardens, tended by more
than twoscore gardeners, included elaborate plantings skillfully designed by a
famous landscape architect and developed under the supervision of an experi-
enced head gardener. Roses, peonies, irises, dahlias, gladioli, lilies, and seemingly all other flowers he had aplenty, and many were the magnificent
specimens we admired. But beyond an interest in garden flowers this American estate owner was absorbed in the hobby of cultivating native flowers, and
of no plant we saw that day was he prouder, and none gave him greater
delight, than a tiny clump of schizaea he had succeeded, after many failures,
in establishing. Schizaea is a rare, frail fern of minute proportions; it is known
as curly grass. A keen perception of values is needed to appreciate the real
satisfaction that the cultivation of such a plant can bring.

Many wildings are as unpretentious as kittens and are loved for their
simplicity, charm, and associations rather than for their showiness; others are
equal in display value to many of the finest garden kinds.

Grow a packet of mixed gourd seed and you may pick a harvest like this. The decorative possibilities with gourds are endless. Use them in centerpieces or handicraft projects. Publications of the Gourd Society of America have disseminated much responsible information on gourd culture and history.

The grower of wild flowers is usually a lover of the fields, woods, streamsides, and hills; his way takes him across the paths of naturalists and botanists; he is likely to learn a great deal more about his plants than merely how to grow them. He reaps a twofold pleasure from his hobby; the one, the joy of growing plants, some of which are tantalizingly capricious, the other the satisfaction of searching for and observing wildings in their native haunts. Being a true lover of nature, the wild-flower gardener is a conservationist; he dedicates himself to the preservation of the native flora and does all he can to prevent its spoliation and destruction.

Rock gardening claims the attentions of many amateurs. Its fascinations are closely akin to those of wild gardening because a good rock garden is an epitome of nature and a good rock gardener a close student of the ways of plants in the wild. Unlike the native plant specialist, the rock gardener does not restrict himself to denizens of his own continent, country, or floristic area; he is interested in all small, choice plants, no matter from which part of the world they come, provided they are likely to be suitable for his purpose and hardy in his locality. Although he does not confine himself geographically, he limits the size and general character of the plants he admits to his

66

Though native habitats of wild flowers are decreasing, wild flowers, paradoxically, are on the increase. Nurseries specialize in their propagation, and gardeners can buy plants that will thrive under the right cultural conditions. Many areas, such as Bartholomew's Cobble, in Massachusetts, have been set aside as wild-flower preserves and the public has become aware of conservation efforts through garden clubs and groups such as the Wild Flower Preservation Society.

domain—most are mountain plants or at least look as though they might be mountain plants, and so are dwarf or low and exquisite.

The rock gardener deals with gems, and like the jeweler is as much concerned with their settings as with the treasures themselves. A choice ramonda clinging and blooming in a north-facing vertical crevice, a Himalayan androsace spreading strawberry-like, but less overpoweringly along a stone-chip-covered ledge, or a cheerful but tiny *Primula rosea* flowering beside a streamlet gives him joy indeed. But less exacting plants, well placed, do so too; what more lovely or dependable than crowded rosettes of the cobweb houseleek, *Sempervivum arachnoideum,* or than the golden stars of *Anemone ranunculoides* in early spring?

The pleasure of the rock gardener does not end with admiring the beauty of the plants he grows or the charm of the settings he creates or develops for them or even from growing his plants. He gets great satisfaction too from the intimate knowledge he gleans of his plants and their needs. Each is a distinct personality; each has a fascinating history. He knows their origins, their relatives, their likes and dislikes, and something of the circumstances of their discovery or development and of their native habitats.

Orchids are the preference of all amateur green-house owners, and even house plant enthusiasts can grow the orchid, *Odontoglossum grande,* as well as others without benefit of greenhouse. Professional and amateur growers may belong to the American Orchid Society.

From late winter until late fall—from the coming of the first snowdrop until *Saxifraga cortusaefolia* blooms, ghostlike, among autumn leaves—the rock garden sustains its owner's interest, then when winter comes, the enthusiast puts his garden to bed, turns to his library shelves, and travels vicariously with Farrer, Forrest, Ward, Elliot, and other great plant hunters who have ranged the mountains of the world seeking worth-while alpine plants.

I know a businessman who, on a suburban acre near New York, has created a wonderful and exquisitely beautiful rock garden. Over a period of years he has developed natural rock outcrops and has extended and planted them sympathetically. Despite marvelous restraint (and that is essential in good rock gardening) a fabulous number of rare, choice plants are at home and thriving in this small garden, and its owner knows them all.

His garden provides this man with an absorbing distraction from the cares of business and gives pleasure not only to him but to the many rock-garden enthusiasts who from time to time visit it. And giving pleasure to others is a joy and privilege that comes to most garden hobbyists.

Over the greater part of the country active gardening outdoors ceases with the coming of winter; it is then that indoor gardening comes into special

While the die-hard gladiolus fancier strives for bigger and bigger spikes, Mr. Average Gardener is growing both miniature (shown here) and baby varieties (two distinct types). Three groups, the National Gladiolus Society, the New England Gladiolus Society, and the North American Gladiolus Council, serve the interests of hobbyists.

prominence, although it is done throughout the year. Indoor gardening includes both the cultivation of plants in rooms and in greenhouses; it is the only gardening that the shut-in, the invalid, and many aged people can usually do.

The cultivation of house plants has always made a very special appeal. From earliest days housewives have grown cherished specimens in their windows and have exchanged slips and rooted plants with neighbors. Geraniums and fuchsias, patience plants and wandering Jew, English ivy, begonias and the campanula New Englanders call star-of-Bethlehem have long been home favorites.

In recent years a tremendous renascence of interest in tropical plants has occurred and wide varieties of these are now obtainable and are grown in American homes. Not since the latter part of the nineteenth century, when the world was scoured by Europeans for tropical plants to furnish the conservatories of the wealthy, has such a search for good decorative plants from the tropics been made. In the last ten or fifteen years numerous expeditions by Americans have resulted in increasing the already great variety of attractive pot plants that are offered by florists and are obtainable from specialist dealers.

Rocks and plants belong together. Rock gardening is a special part of horticulture, many of its adherents belonging to the American Rock Garden Society.

Engaging catalogues are issued by some commercial growers, and one firm, Julius Roehrs, of East Rutherford, New Jersey, has issued a sumptuous publication of nearly one hundred large-size pages in which nearly fourteen hundred different kinds of tropical and subtropical plants adapted for pot culture are described and illustrated and in which suggestions for their culture are given. This magnificent production is the work of Alfred Byrd Graf, who traveled around the world in his search for new plants adapted for cultivation and decoration in American homes. The fact that the first edition sold out within weeks of its appearance and that plans are now being made for a third edition is indicative of the tremendous interest in these plants.

But pot-plant culture is not limited to exotics. A few years ago Werner Lieb, of New Rochelle, New York, popularized the pick-a-back plant, a native of our Pacific Northwest. He told me that his profits from this effort paid his daughter's expenses through college.

Developments in the greenhouse-building industry, particularly the automatic controls of ventilation, heating, etc., that eliminate tiresome hour-to-hour attention previously required, have made it practical for many more home gardeners to have small glasshouse units than heretofore; if the trend

Though this flower may look like a shaggy dog, it is typical of one class of chrysanthemums, the spider. Spider chrysanthemums, as well as the big exhibition types seen in corsages at football games, have recently been grown by amateurs as well as professionals, largely owing to efforts of enthusiastic members of the National Chrysanthemum Society.

continues we may expect to see the home greenhouse as common in American towns and suburbs as in parts of Europe.

The cultivation of plants indoors, whether in rooms, sunrooms, or greenhouses, provides tremendous thrills and satisfactions. Here as nowhere else the gardener has many environmental factors most completely under control. *He* makes the decisions whether to supply or withhold water, the type of soil to use, when to afford more root room, and, during the cooler parts of the year at least, to what temperatures his plants shall be submitted. Here is controlled cultivation. Here results are least likely to be affected by outside circumstances, by what the insurance companies are pleased to term acts of God.

And so the arts of growing plants indoors and of propagating and raising new sorts are becoming known to many more; it is a healthy development that will surely continue to spread. Modern homes with better-controlled indoor climates and increased window areas expand the possibilities of the many kinds that can be successfully grown.

Thirty million amateur gardeners in America! From Alaska to southernmost Florida, from New York to San Francisco interest in horticulture waxes. What is the significance of this and what are its social implications?

One of the youngest plant organizations is the American Daffodil Society, the first meeting of which took place in the spring of 1954. The yellow variety King Alfred is of the trumpet class, and while there are many other yellow, white, bicolored, or pinkish varieties, this is a consistently reliable one.

Time was when an interest in flowers was considered slightly "sissy," women's business, or perhaps the affectation of the dilettante; men were meant for sterner things. Time was too when gardening lacked the essential respectability it now enjoys. Love of music, of fine literature, of the theater, and of painting was considered commendable. Such interests provided legitimate discussion among the intelligentsia, but gardening was on a lower plane, a matter of less general interest, of much less cultural importance. That is no longer true. Now even those who don't garden recognize its cultural worth.

This new regard has come about slowly, almost imperceptibly. A back-to-the-land movement gained momentum almost without our being aware of the revolution it implied.

Much has been heard of the flow of population and of popular interest from the country to the city, much less of that from the city to the country, yet a tremendous surge in this latter direction has occurred. True, this expansion is less agricultural than horticultural, the new American with his fingers in the dirt is much more likely to tend a suburban lot or a few country acres than a quarter section or more of farm land, but he is just as interested in the soil, its capabilities, and its products as was his agrarian

forefather. He is a gardener, a horticulturist, and horticulture differs from agriculture chiefly in that it is intensive rather than extensive and that it is concerned with a far wider range of kinds of plants.

This changed attitude is a measure of a grown-up civilization. Love of gardens and of gardening has always been a manifestation of mature societies, of assemblages that have sufficient accumulated wealth, leisure, and education to appreciate the truly finer things of life. America's present concern with its soil and the plants that can be grown in it is a sure sign of sanity in a world that at times seems slightly insane.

III

A GARDENER'S
STORY OF THE SOIL

by Montague Free

SOIL is a living, dynamic thing, capable of being improved or of being misused to the point of ruination. It consists of many things: of rock fragments of varying size; of plant and animal remains, in various stages of decay, which ultimately disintegrate to form humus; of living organisms that play their part in breaking down and building up plant nutrients and add to the store of organic matter; of the soil solution; of gaseous elements. Truly the soil is living and dynamic—but it is much more than that. It is the source from which plants get essential nutrients. And without plants there could be no animals—no insects or spiders, no fish or birds, no you or me.

The making of soil fit for the nourishment of higher plants and animals was no overnight job. It began a long time ago, and Mother Earth took an immeasurable time in doing it. But a picture, sketchy though it must be, of how she went about the business of making this life-giving soil, and of how its fertility is lost and regained should provide for every gardener a fuller and a better understanding of how to husband properly the soil provided for us.

"In the beginning," we read, ". . . the earth was without form, and void." As the mass began to cool, the oceans took shape. And as the waters receded and the rocks emerged, various soil-making agencies—frost and fire, wind and rain, the rise and fall of temperature—began their role in breaking down the rocks into fragments. These, by presenting a greater surface to weathering, broke down ever more quickly, thus aiding in the production of the dissolved minerals that form a vital part of our soils today. Fiery volcanoes, vomiting lava, cinders, and volcanic ash, provided, as they still provide, soil-making materials that weathered more rapidly still.

These disintegration processes that were in operation at the dawn of creation are still going on. Wind and rain, running water, and ice still play a part in soil making. I have a friend whose work requires considerable driving in a wind-swept area along the shore of the ocean. Replacement of the windshield of his car is sometimes necessary as a result of the abrasive action of the wind-carried sand, which converts it into a semi-opaque ground glass. A more spectacular illustration of wind as a soil-making agent is to be seen in parts of the West, where wind-borne sand cuts away the soft material of rock masses, leaving the more resistant portions in the form of fantastic pillars.

The greatest solvent in nature is water, and it very slowly affects even the hardest rocks, especially when they are broken into tiny fragments. It contributes to the physical breakdown of rocks also, to a very minor degree, by the battering force of raindrops and, to a great degree, as running water. Its flow may carry with it rock particles or even boulders that, as they are transported, exercise tremendous grinding power on other rocks in the stream or gully bed. The Grand Canyon of the Colorado is one of many examples of the grinding, erosive effects of running water. In course of time plant life played an increasing part in soil making, by breaking rocks apart. The young root of a tree, finding a tiny crevice in a rock, follows it along, gets enough nutrients to enable it to grow, increase in diameter, and exercise enough disruptive force to split the rock. Maybe some of you have had a cellar wall injured by the invasive roots of a poplar working along similar lines.

Changes in temperature are as effective as the hammer of the convict on the stone pile in breaking up rocks of certain types. When the minerals composing the rocks expand unequally under the influence of heat, they readily disintegrate by alternate heating and cooling. Some of you may have solved the problem of moving a boulder too large to handle as a whole by building a fire around it and then, when the rock is good and hot, throwing over it several pailfuls of cold water. This is a spectacular and comparatively easy way to break up some kinds of rocks into fragments small enough to handle. It is conceivable that a forest fire followed by rain might have a similar effect on rocks in its path. Hot days that warm the rocks throughout, followed by cold nights that cool the outer layer first and cause it to contract over the still-expanded core, may result in surface scaling analogous to the way a buttonwood sheds its bark.

When the water contained in rock crevices is frozen, the expansion that accompanies the change of water into ice may be sufficient to split off segments of rock; these in rolling down a slope may break and grind other rocks with which they come in contact, or may themselves be broken into smaller pieces. The pursuit of happiness leads me to travel rather frequently on a railroad whose tracks often pass through rock cuts. In the spring it is always possible to observe clean, fresh rock surfaces here and there where hunks have been pried off as a result of the freezing of water in cracks.

The milky streams seen issuing from glaciers are visual evidence of the power of these huge ice masses ever moving forward and carrying with them embedded in the ice rocks of various sizes that scrape the rocky floor beneath them with immense pressure and irresistible force. So the ground rock becomes flour, to color the glacial streams. The glaciers that formerly covered much of North America played a large part in helping to form the basic soils of our Northern states.

There are still other mechanical agencies that help in soil making. The tillage tools of the farmer, the spade and hoe of the gardener, the burrowing activities of soil-inhabiting animals—the conies, woodchucks, mice and moles, ground beetles, and earthworms—all play a part, though perhaps a minor one, in disintegrating rocks and rock fragments and, by making them smaller, expose greater surface areas to the action of other agencies that will ultimately result in their decomposition and in the production of a soil.

The breaking of rocks into dust is only part of the story. We must go back again to the beginnings of life to look at the part played by living things and chemical agencies in soil building that through aeons have brought the good earth to that stage where it is capable of supporting animal life.

Our picture of the first living organisms is purely speculative. Pooh-Bah (the Lord High Everything Else of Gilbert and Sullivan's *Mikado*), who was a man of great family pride, traced his lineage back to a "protoplasmal, primordial atomic globule." Probably the first entities to have the spark of life were akin to Pooh-Bah's globule: microscopic organisms floating in water, able to thrive on air, water, and the salts dissolved in it, and having an outlook on life similar to that of some of the present-day bacteria. Possibly from these primitive organisms there developed minute one-celled plants able to manufacture chlorophyll and still existing by floating in the sea. As the waters receded and exposed the rocks, land plants appeared—perhaps Algae similar to the single-celled Pleurococcus, which smears tree trunks and fences with a film of living green.

Developing along with these primitive plants were the progenitors of the animal kingdom, perhaps one-celled animals along the lines of our present-day amoebas, preying upon the plants because they, like the higher animals (including man), are unable to get a living from air, water, and mineral salts, but are absolutely dependent for food upon organic matter built up by plant life. These primitive organisms, plant and animal, passed through the well-known cycle of birth, life, and death, and in dying made their contribution to one of the most important components of the soil—organic matter. And so the Creator made the world ready for the beginning of the evolution of plant and animal life, which was later to make the earth a place suited to the development of mankind.

It is now time we took another look at Pooh-Bah's "protoplasmal, primordial, atomic globule." From it, as we have seen, simple organisms developed which were able to manufacture chlorophyll, that miraculous substance which makes it possible for plants to use the energy of sunlight in breaking down carbon dioxide (carbonic-acid gas) and in building up carbon compounds such as sugars and starches.

These grandfathers of all life were the Algae: their descendants are with us today—some, the seaweeds, still occupying their native element, from which it is believed all life originally came; some growing in river and brook, lake, pond, or puddle; some in and on the soil; and some which mar or embellish, according to the point of view, the flowerpots in which we grow our house plants.

As conditions became more favorable for plant life, the Fungi developed—plants without chlorophyll, which are able to live on decaying organic matter—and these added their quota to the organic matter of the developing soil. Along with them came the Lichens, a co-operative enterprise of Algae and Fungi. The Lichens perched on rocks and dissolved minerals from their hosts. In dying they left a legacy of nutrients for the liverworts and mosses, the next stage in development. These have chlorophyll but no true roots; they absorb the moisture necessary for existence by root hairs known as rhizoids.

In order to live on "dry" land, roots were necessary to absorb moisture from the soil and, as the plants began to grow in stature, to anchor them. The first plants with roots were club mosses and horsetails, and these during the Carboniferous period grew to gigantic size. This was the age of the giant amphibians, "some of which were almost as big as donkeys." It was during this time that most of the coal measures were laid down by the accumulation of spores and debris of club-moss forests.

This is not the place to trace the evolution through the ferns, cycads, and cone-bearers to the flowering plants as we know them today. The point is that as vegetation increased in luxuriance, so did animal life multiply, and when these living organisms, animal and vegetable, died, their remains, with the minerals they had built into their bodies, were returned to Mother Earth to add to the store of organic matter in the soil where it provides food for other plants and animals—bacteria, fungi, actinomyces, protozoa, algae, earthworms, June bugs, Japanese beetles, seventeen-year locusts, nematodes, and what not, all of which help to bring about the decomposition of organic matter to form humus—a never-ending cycle of birth, life, death, decay, rebirth.

During these processes of decay the carbon is broken down to carbonic-acid gas (the soil air contains ten times as much carbon dioxide as the air we breathe and from which plants obtain their supply of carbon), some of which escapes to the air and some of which combines with the soil water to form carbonic acid. The plant and animal proteins, through a series of extremely complex operations, are changed to simpler compounds by the action of myriads of tiny organisms (a thimbleful of rich soil is said to contain a billion or more of them). These chemical changes follow an orderly progression. Ammonia is formed, some of which may be lost in the air as gas, some taken up by higher plants, some seized by denitrifying bacteria and liberated as gaseous nitrogen, and some taken up by nitrite bacteria and converted into nitrites. The nitrites in turn are seized upon by nitrate bacteria and converted into nitrates, in which nitrogen occurs in a form readily available as a nutrient for our plants.

Living plant roots, too, excrete carbonic acid, which combines with bases to produce carbonates or bicarbonates. The iron in the minerals oxidizes in the presence of air and water; minerals unite with water to form hydrates; minerals containing base elements may exchange part of the base with hydrogen from water. These chemical reactions, often rather complicated, are continually in progress in moist soils and are important factors in bringing about the decomposition of the raw materials from which soils are made.

And so a soil is born. Uncountable years have gone into its make-up; life, death, decay, and rebirth have played their part. We, too, must play our part and work the soil with reverence and a full appreciation of the fact that a few years of abuse, neglect, and mishandling can tear down and destroy that which nature has so tirelessly built up.

The better to comprehend the proper management of soil, it is helpful to know something of how plants get a living and soils lose fertility.

Our crop plants today, the ornamental plants grown in our gardens, our forests and lawns belong in highly specialized groups needing something more than to be immersed in a saline solution and have access to carbonic acid to enable them to thrive, as did the first seaweeds.

Sunshine and rain, air and soil, all are necessary for the natural growth of higher plants, whether they be radishes or roses. Living plants contain about 75 per cent water, which is taken up by the roots from the soil. Apart from being the source of the hydrogen content of plants, it serves as transportation system for carrying minerals in solution from the soil and for moving from place to place within the plant the elaborate food materials manufactured by it. The provision of an adequate supply of water therefore is obvious. It must be in the soil in a quantity usable by plants—not too much and not too little.

This leaves us with about 25 per cent solid material. Does this all come from the soil? The answer is, no. The dry matter of plants consists of 50 per cent more of carbon. This they obtain from the air in the form of carbon dioxide, which with water, by a series of steps, is recombined by the chlorophyll with the aid of sunlight into sugars and starches, and some of its oxygen is liberated in the form of gas. Even though carbon is present in the air to the extent of only .03 per cent (or three parts in ten thousand), we do not have to worry about maintaining a supply of it, for it is enough and is constantly replenished by the exhalations of animals and as a product of the decay of organic materials.

About 40 per cent of the dry matter is made up of hydrogen and oxygen obtained from water and air, and the remaining 10 per cent consists of nitrogen, phosphorus, potash, calcium, sulphur, iron, magnesium, in varying proportions, together with "minor" or "trace" elements, such as manganese, boron, copper, and zinc. These are acquired in solution from the soil, and although they form only a small percentage of the total weight of the living plant, they are important.

Our job is to insure that there is no avoidable loss of these nutrients and to till the soil so that water and nutrients are available for plants growing in it. Before we can do this intelligently, we must know how fertility is lost.

It is generally conceded that our soils on the whole are less fertile than they used to be. This concerns all of us—butcher, baker, candlestick maker, and especially the farmer and gardener. Some of the loss of soil fertility is unavoidable, some occurs only under conditions of extensive culture and hence more nearly concerns the agriculturist than the gardener, but knowing how nutrients are lost helps us all toward an understanding of proper soil management.

Plants take from the soil nitrogen, phosphorus, potash, calcium, and a host of lesser elements. When crops are removed from the soil, it is poorer to the extent of nutrients contained in them. When crop removal is in the form of human foodstuffs—potatoes, onions, wheat, parsnips, and what not —and consumed in large cities, the fertility is lost for a long time to come because of modern methods in the disposal of town wastes that incinerate garbage and send sewage on its way to the sea. When crops are eaten by farm animals, part of the fertility is returned in their excrement, while that part which goes into the building of their bodies is mostly lost to the soil (except for bones, blood, and so on, made into fertilizer), for we in turn eat the animals, and when our time comes, the disposition of our bodies is such that they make little or no contribution to soil fertility.

Soluble nutrients may be lost to the surface layer by leaching to lower levels or by being carried away by drainage water, which ultimately reaches lakes, ponds, and the ocean. Some of these nutrients may be returned to the soil when fish scrap, seaweed, and pond mud are used for fertilizer. A vast proportion of them are lost forever so far as we are concerned.

Wind can carry away topsoil in clouds and result in "dust bowl" conditions. Some of the dust falls to augment the fertility of other soils, but much of it may be carried out to sea and lost.

A heavy rain can carry off an incredible amount of the most fertile part of the soil by what is known as sheet erosion. When the topography is such that the runoff water becomes concentrated in channels, gully erosion results. These water-carried soils, when they finally come to rest, as in river deltas, may develop into areas suitable for crop production.

When organic matter is burned, the nitrogen contained in it reverts to its gaseous form, and it may be a long, long time before it is returned to the soil. The destruction by fire of humus and organic matter, fresh or in various stages of decay, not only results in the loss of the plant nutrients, but also deprives the soil of materials needed for maintaining a favorable soil structure and for providing the right conditions for the microorganisms concerned with the maintenance of soil fertility. Naked and exposed burned-over areas are subject to further loss by wind and water erosion until such time as other vegetation comes in to start once more the cycle of building up a fertile soil.

A certain amount of loss in one or more of these ways is inevitable and indeed not undesirable. It may be compared to exchange and barter and the circulation of money. Soils are still being made, and nutrients are still going into solution to make up for inevitable losses. Our problem is to maintain a balance between income and outgo by good husbandry. This in the larger sense may involve resting the land by taking it out of cultivation, which is done by maintaining a semi-permanent cover of vegetation that may be forest or grass; and by strip cropping and rotations in which pasture occupies the ground for longer periods than cultivated crops. Forest and deep-rooting crops in general are considered to be especially desirable for rehabilitating soil because their deeply penetrating roots bring up nutrients from the lower levels.

Of more immediate concern to the home gardener is the problem as it affects him. His two-by-four plot is influenced by some or all of the factors that control the fertility of the land as a whole. What can he do to prevent loss of fertility and maintain an adequate supply of nutrients?

Now we are concerned largely with the practical application of measures designed to prevent the loss of fertility and to build up depleted soils—and why.

We can't do much about the loss of nutrients by crop removal, except to compost all the vegetable wastes we can lay our hands on, and then return them to the soil when they are partly or wholly decayed.

Loss by leaching and by wind and water erosion can, to a large extent, be prevented by the use of cover crops during these periods when the land is vacant. A cover of vegetation absorbs soluble nutrients that might otherwise depart in the drainage water, and its mass of roots prevents the topsoil from being washed or blown bodily away. The top growth, too, helps prevent blowing and softens the eroding effect of beating rains. If cover crops are turned under when they are green, they quickly decay, and the nutrients in them help the crop which follows.

In order to build up an exhausted soil it is necessary to incorporate ample amounts of organic matter to replenish its content of humus. This may be in the form of decayed or partly decayed manure, compost, leafmold, peat moss, or cover crops turned under as "green manure." It may be necessary, or at least desirable, to "prime the pump" by fertilizing the cover crop with a complete commercial fertilizer to insure the growth of a sufficient bulk of vegetation to make a worth-while addition of organic matter.

So far as fire is concerned, the gardener can deprive himself of the "nostalgic fires of autumn" and instead put tree leaves and garden trash on the compost pile.

The fertility of soil is contingent upon a number of interrelated factors, one of the most important of which is moisture. Poorly drained soils are unsuited for garden use, except for the growth of bog and swamp plants. When they are poorly drained, they become waterlogged. When water drives out the air, roots become unhealthy, and the growth of the fungi and micro-organisms that are largely responsible for soil fertility is prevented. The chemical activity of the soil is greatly slowed down because the oxidation of minerals cannot take place in the absence of air. When waterlogging is caused by an impervious hardpan just below the surface, which prevents water from percolating to the subsoil and, as a corollary, prevents water from rising by capillarity from lower levels, a paradoxical situation may develop: the soil may be too wet during rainy periods, and yet the plants may suffer from drought much earlier than they would in a well-drained soil.

In order to insure favorable water relations unwanted water must be quickly removed and, contrariwise, its absorption facilitated when needed. The first is accomplished by artificial drainage whenever it is necessary. When poor drainage is caused by a relatively thin hardpan, breaking it up by means of a subsoil plow or even by deep digging may be all that is needed.

Measures that help insure the penetration of rain and prevent runoff (with consequent loss, not only of precious water, but equally precious topsoil) include contour culture or terracing and protection of the surface from beating rains that quickly destroy the crumb structure (more of this later) so that water tends to run off rather than to be absorbed. This last end is achieved in part by keeping the ground fully occupied with crops during the periods when heavy rains are expected, by mulches, by the maintenance of plentiful supplies of organic materials in the surface layer, and by the encouragement of earthworms through whose tunnels water finds entrance to lower levels.

The soil must breathe. The importance of proper aeration must be recognized. Not only is it necessary for the healthy growth of roots, for chemical activity, and for the well-being of desirable microorganisms, but also to prevent the formation of substances harmful or poisonous to plants that occurs under airless conditions. (A slightly technical example is the reduction of sulphates to sulphites, whereby the toxic hydrogen sulphide, with its characteristic rotten-egg odor, is produced.) Aeration is primarily a matter of adequate underdrainage.

Heavy clay soils are more likely to be in need of aeration than sandy soils. Under garden conditions the texture of a heavy soil can be improved and made more porous by the incorporation of coarse sand or of coal ashes with the dust sifted out. Bulky organic matter—strawy manure, partly decayed leaves, and so on—is helpful when mixed with heavy soil because, as decomposition proceeds, it shrinks in bulk, leaving air spaces. The development of a granular structure and tillage by digging and plowing and cultivating to break the surface crust also aid in aeration.

But an adequate supply of nutrients and moisture and an adequate aeration are only part of the soil's story. These are tied up with its physical nature—meaning its texture and structure—which has an important bearing on the success or failure of plants.

The texture of a soil is determined by the size of the particles forming it. In sandy soil many of the particles are large enough to be plainly visible but in clay they are so small that they cannot be differentiated with the naked eye. The size of the particles is of double-barreled importance in affecting both the physical nature of the soil and the amount of available nutrients. It can easily be seen that the nutrients can more readily go into solution in clay than in sand because of the greater area exposed to the action of soil water. This can be demonstrated by dissolving two pieces of rock candy of equal size, one pounded into fragments, the other unbroken. Stir them both in water and see which lot of sugar dissolves first.

On the physical side the pore spaces between the particles of sand are larger than those of clay, and consequently they admit air more freely and drain more rapidly. Clay soils may be so dense that they are impervious alike to water, air, and plant roots.

Structure is the term applied to the arrangement of the soil particles. The structure may be single-grained or compound. A compound structure in which the particles adhere in clusters, giving the soil a granular or crumblike formation, is desirable from the standpoint of the farmer and gardener. (In clay soils the clusters formed from the finer particles may be so small that they are invisible to the naked eye.)

There are many factors that tend to influence soil structure. Working heavy, sticky soils when they are wet may destroy the desirable granular or compound structure, which is the reason garden authorities are always so insistent that you should never work the soil when it is wet enough to stick to the tools. Much tramping has the same bad effect. On the other hand, alternate freezing and thawing and alternate wetting and drying are effective in transforming intractable clods from a pasty mass to a friable, granular structure. One reason for plowing heavy soils in the fall is to expose them more fully to the action of frost, which, by expanding water into ice, breaks up the clods. Plant roots in various ways bring about a granular structure—by forcing their way among soil particles, by root secretions, and by the withdrawal of water from soil colloids, which results finally in cementing particles together. Perhaps one of the reasons why gardeners prefer to use sods from a pasture as a base for potting soil is the granular structure induced by the roots of grasses.

The application of lime sticks the particles of sandy soils together and has a granulating or "flocculating" tendency when applied to clay soils.

Last but not least, organic matter has a profound influence. In a coarse, partly decayed state it is of great assistance in opening up heavy clay soils. As decomposition proceeds, it shrinks in bulk, leaving air spaces, and when it is more fully decayed to form humus, its colloidal properties have the effect of cementing particles together—especially important in the case of sandy soils.

Clay soils are very difficult to work, sticky when wet, and inclined to bake into hard intractable clods when dry. Because they hold water with tenacity, they warm up slowly and cannot be worked early in spring because of their wetness. Usually they are rich in fertility, which may be unavailable because of unfavorable water relations.

On the other hand, sandy soils are easy to work, and they warm up quickly in the spring, which provides a couple of reasons why they are in favor with truck farmers and market gardeners who like to make an early start and raise a succession of crops each year. It is the porosity that permits the quick drainage away of water in the surface layer and consequent quicker warming. This, in turn, makes it possible to work the ground earlier in the spring. The lack of retentiveness, however, is a handicap during dry spells. The comparatively large size of the particles makes them rather inactive chemically, and in consequence they tend toward a lack of available nutrients.

Light sandy soils, then, can be improved by the addition of organic matter, preferably rotted manure, in liberal quantities. This will help to hold moisture, add nutrients, and by its further decomposition help dissolve the mineral elements contained in the sand. The basic colloidal part of the humus will tend to hold the particles together, develop a crumb structure, and further help to hold moisture. Lime, as we have seen, also helps to cement the particles together and should be used if the soil is on the acid side. Sandy soils should be provided with a cover crop in winter to hold available nutrients and thus prevent loss by leaching and to prevent loss of topsoil by wind erosion.

Garden soils usually consist of a mixture of sand, silt, and clay (along with organic matter) in varying proportions. When they are about equal, the soil is termed loam. When one or other of the types predominates, it is distinguished as sandy loam, silt loam, or clay loam, as the case may be. There are other finer distinctions, but we need not bother with them here. Average garden soils are easier to handle than extreme types. When they are on the heavy side, the management suitable for clay soils is indicated; when they are light, that applicable to sandy soils should be used.

The importance of adequate supplies of organic matter in all soils cannot be overemphasized. Not only does it supply the essential element, nitrogen, and return nutrient minerals to the soil in a form soon ready to be absorbed by growing plants, but during the processes of decay acids are released that, in contact with the mineral particles of the soil, help to dissolve them. As in unbalanced soils it also improves the physical condition of the soil, and helps to prevent the leaching of nutrients.

Deep preparation of the soil aids aeration, helps to insure the free passage of gravitational water and a reservoir of moisture. There is a saying in England that the good gardener digs his soil an inch deeper every year: seldom, however, is the soil dug more than three feet deep—presumably after the expiration of thirty years the soil is sufficiently built up and the gardener is worn out! Enthusiasm for deep preparation should not impel anyone to reverse topsoil and subsoil (trenching) until the latter has been improved by adding humus for several years.

To sum it all up: Nature has, through the ages, built up a system for the constant use and replenishment and reuse of the earth by growing things. Man has managed to develop a speed-up of the whole basic process, with emphasis on the use and reuse. So man must—if he is wise, and a good gardener—emphasize the replenishment, too, and see to it that the earth is kept ever fit and ready to do its best work.

IV

A PICTORIAL
GARDEN CALENDAR

THE TWELVE FURBER PRINTS
FROM COLONIAL WILLIAMSBURG

IN 1730 an English nurseryman named Robert Furber conceived a new idea for a seed catalogue and wrote a book that he decorated with twelve copper engravings of flower arrangements.

He called his publication *Twelve Months of Flowers*. Today, after more than two hundred years, his book is still in use.

Today's flower lovers find the eighteenth-century book valuable, not for its gardening tips, but for its pictures. The twelve colored prints in the book show suitable flower arrangements for each month of the year.

The flowers pictured in Furber's prints are botanically accurate and are arranged according to the month in which they may be seen. Furber provided a key with each of his twelve pictures, indexing the flowers with a number and their names.

In the eighteenth century patrons actually ordered their new plant materials after studying the prints. More than four hundred flowers are shown in the engravings, which Furber described as being "colored from life."

One set of Furber's prints is displayed in Williamsburg, Virginia, in the historic George Wythe House, where they grace the staircase wall. Colonial Williamsburg, Incorporated, which restored Williamsburg to its eighteenth-century setting, owns the prints plus a 1732 issue of another Furber book called

The Flower Garden Displayed. Visitors to Williamsburg are able to buy reproductions of the prints.

The second book contains the same set of prints. Furber, in his second publication, said he thought the prints would be valuable to both gardeners and ladies interested in water colors. The prints, he hoped, would also wipe out a mistaken idea that flowers were not available in winter months. He pictured at least thirty-two blooming in the winter.

Furber's prints have served as a guide to Colonial Williamsburg's flower lady, Mrs. Louise B. Fisher, who makes the colonial flower arrangements decorating Williamsburg's exhibition buildings. She has found it impossible to use all the flowers Furber prescribes for each month. Some of them do not grow in Virginia and some have a different season than in England.

Opposite each print, reproduced here through the courtesy of Colonial Williamsburg, you will find listed the flowers shown in the arrangement. The original spellings have been retained, some varying from current English usage (for example, "blew" for the color blue). Some are of varieties no longer seen, but most of the flowers can be picked out by a good eye. Generally the flowers first on the list are near the center of the arrangement, and as you go down the list you'll find them by going clockwise, often in an outward spiral.

JANUARY

Pellitory with daisy flowers, Winter Aconite, Great early Snow drop, Single Snow drop, White edged Polyanthos, Double Peach Colou'd Hepatica, Double blew Violet, Winter blew Hyacinth, Lesser black Hellebore, Dwarf white King Spear, Ilex leav'd Jasmine, Red Spring Cyclamen, Acacia or sweet button tree, White Cyclamen, Creeping Borage or Bugloss, Strip'd Spurge, Lisbon Lemmon tree, Canary Campanula, Dwarf Tithymall, Double Stock, Filberd tree in flower, True Venetian Vetch, Seville Orange, Grey Aloe, Winter white Hyacinth, Spotted Aloe, Narrow curl'd leav'd Bay, Tree Savory, Triangle Yellow Ficoides, Strip'd Orange, Strip'd Candy tuft, Tree Sedum, Single blew Anemone.

1. Pellitory with daisy flowers.	9. Lesser black Hellebore.	17. Lisbon Lemmon tree.	25. Winter white Hyacinth.
2. Winter Aconite.	10. Dwarf white King Spear.	18. Canary Campanula.	26. Spotted Aloe.
3. Great early Snow drop.	11. Ilex leav'd Jasmine.	19. Dwarf Sichymall.	27. Narrow curl'd leav'd Bay.
4. Single Snow drop.	12. Red Spring Cyclamen.	20. Double Stock.	28. Triangle Yellow Ficoides.
5. White edged Polyanthos.	13. Acacia or sweet button tree.	21. Filberd tree in flower.	29. Strip'd Orange.
6. Double Peach colour Hepatica.	14. White Cyclamen.	22. True Venetian Vetch.	30. Strip'd Orange.
7. Double blew Violet.	15. Creeping Borage or Bugloss.	23. Seville Orange.	31. Strip'd Candy tuft.
8. Winter blew Hyacinth.	16. Strip'd Spurge.	24. Grey Aloe.	32. Tree Sedum.
			33. Single blew Anemone.

JANUARY

Design'd by P.r Casteels.

From the Collection of Rob.t Furber Gardiner at Kensington. 1730.

Engrav'd by H. Fletcher.

97

FEBRUARY

Duke Vantol Tulip, Silver Edg'd Alaternus, Yellow bloach'd Alaternus, Cornelian Cherry, White Mezereon, Red Mezereon, Double Narcissus of Constantinople, Single Anemone Purple & White, Venetian Vetch true, Double blew Hepatica, Early white Hyacinth, Blush red Dens Caninus, Spring Cyclamen white Edg'd, Strip'd & Edg'd Polyanthus, Single white Hepatica, Single blew Hepatica, White Den Caninus, Double Peach colour'd Hepatica, The greater Snow-drop, White Crocus, Double Snow-drop, Small yellow Crocus, Great blew Crocus, Small blew Crocus, Single dark-red Anemone, Pantaloon strip'd Polyanthus, Persian Iris, Yellow dutch Crocus, Scotch white-strip'd Crocus, Blew Hyacinth Passtout, Fruit bearing Almond, Single Prusian blew Anemone, Yellow Colutea, Peach colour'd single Hepatica, Double Pilewort.

1 *Duke Vantol Tulip.*	9 *Venetian Vetch, true*	18 *Double Peach colour'd Hepatica*	27 *Persian Iris.*
2 *Silver Edg.d Maternus.*	10 *Double blew Hepatica.*	19 *The greater Snow-drop.*	28 *Yellow dutch Crocus.*
3 *Yellow bloch Maternus.*	11 *Early white Hyacinth.*	20 *White Crocus.*	29 *Scotch white strip'd Crocus.*
4 *Cornelian Cherry.*	12 *Blush red Dens Caninus.*	21 *Double Snow-drop.*	30 *Blew Hyacinth Passtoute.*
5 *White Mezereon.*	13 *Spring Cyclamen white Edg.d*	22 *Small yellow Crocus.*	31 *Fruit bearing Almond.*
6 *Red Mezereon.*	14 *Strip'd & Edg.d Polyanthos.*	23 *Great blew Crocus.*	32 *Single Prussian blew Anemones.*
Double Narcissus.	15 *Single white Hepatica.*	24 *Small blew Crocus.*	33 *Yellow Colutea.*
7 *of Constantinople.*	16 *Single blew Hepatica.*	25 *Single dark red Anemone.*	34 *Peach colour'd Single Hepatica.*
8 *Single Anemone Purple & White.*	17 *White Dens Caninus.*	26 *Pantaloon strip'd Polyanthos.*	35 *Double Pilewort.*

FEBRUARY

Design'd by P.r Casteels.

From the Collection of Rob.t Furber Gardiner at Kensington. 1730.

Engrav'd by H. Fletcher.

99

MARCH

Royal Widow Auricula, Dwarf white starry Hyacinth, White Boslamon Narciss, High Admiral Anemone, Rhyven Narciss, White passe flower, White grape flower, The lesser black Hellebore, Danae Auricula, White flowering Almond, Dwarf blew starry Hyacinth, American flowering Maple, Goldfinch Polyanthos, Larger blew starry Hyacinth, Virginian flowering Maple, Narciss of Naples, Best Claremon Tulip, The checker'd Futillaria, Large leav'd Norway Maple, Double pulchra Hyacinth, Queen of France Narciss, Palto Auriflame Tulip, Blew Oriental Hyacinth, Single bloody Wall, Admiral blew Anemone, Bell Baptice Anemone, Monument Anemone, Red flowering Larch tree, Blew passe flower, Rose Jonker Anemone, White flowering Larch tree, Purple strip'd Anemone, The Velvet Iris, Jerusalem Cowslip.

100

1	Royal Widow Auricula.	10 White flowering Almond.	19 Large leav'd Norway Maple.	27 Monument Anemone.
2	Dwarf white starry Hyacinth.	11 Dwarf blew starry Hyacinth.	20 Double pulchra Hyacinth.	28 Red flowering Larch tree.
3	White Boslamon Narciss.	12 American flowering Maple.	21 Queen of France Narciss.	29 Blew passe flower.
4	High Admiral Anemone.	13 Goldfinch Polyanthos.	22 Palto Auri flame Tulip.	30 Rose Jonker Anemone.
5	Rhyren Narciss.	14 Larger blew starry Hyacinth.	23 Blew Orientab Hyacinth.	31 White flowering Larch tree.
6	White passe flower.	15 Virginian flowering Maple.	24 Single bloody Wall.	32 Purple strip'd Anemone.
7	White grape flower.	16 Narciss of Naples.	25 Admiral blew Anemone.	33 The Velvet Iris.
8	The lesser black Helleboro.	17 Best Claremon Tulip.	26 Bell Baptice Anemone.	34 Jerusalem Conslip.
9	Danae Auricula.	18 The checker'd Futillaria.		

MARCH

Design'd by P. Casteels.   From the Collection of Rob.t Furber Gardener at Kensington. 1730.   Engrav'd by H. Fletcher.

101

APRIL

Keysers Jewel Hyacinth, Diamond do [ditto], Double blossom'd Peach, Single Orange Narcissus, Double Endroit Tulip, Glory of Ye East Auricula, Double Wall flower, Blush red lilly of ye vally. British King Anemone, Calestis Anemone Amaranthus trachee, Single Junquill, Loves Master Auricula, Double painted Lady Auricula, Palurus Christs thorn, White Lilly of the Vally, Merveille du Monde Auricula, Lady Margareta Anemone, Juliana do. [ditto], Double Junquill, Duke of Beauford Auricula, Lecreep No. 1 Tulip, Beau Regard Tulip, Dwarf Single flowering Almond, Duke of St. Albans Auricula, Turky ranunculus sweet scented, Double Cuckow Flower, Grand Presence Auricula, Sea Pink, Double flowering Almond.

1 Keysers Jewel Hyacinth.	9 British King Anemone.	17 Merveille du Monde Auricula. — Almond.
2 Diamend d.°	10 Cælestis Anemone.	18 Lady Margareta Anemone 25 Duke of St Alban Auricula
3 Double blossom'd Peach.	11 Amaranthus trachee.	19 Tiliana d.° 26 Turky ranunculus sweet
4 Single Orange Narcissus.	12 Single Junquill.	20 Double Junquill. Scented
5 Double Endroit Tulip.	13 Loves Master Auricula.	21 Leericp. N.° 1 Tulip. 27 Double Cuckow Flower
6 Glory of y.° East Auricula.	14 Double painted Lady Auricula.	22 Leericp. N.° 1 Tulip. 28 Grand Presence Auricula
7 Double Wall flower.	15 Palurus Christs thorn.	23 Beau Regard Tulip. 29 Sea Pink.
8 Blush red lilly of y.° Vally.	16 White lilly of the Vally.	24 Dwarf Single flowering— 30 Double flowering Almond.

APRIL

Desin'd by Pet.r Casteels.

From the Collection of Rob.t Furber Gardiner, at Kensington 1730.

Engrav'd by H.r Fletcher.

MAY

Cinamon Rose, Narrow Leav'd Strip'd flower de-
luce, Columbine Strip'd Bishop of Canterbury
Tulip, Double Catch fly, Late white Hyacinth, Blew
bell Hyacinth, Mountain bulbed crow foot, Belsilvia
Anemone, Venetian Vetch, Blew Hyacinth of Peru,
China pink, Savoy Spider wort, Double Orange
Lilly, White Hyacinth of Peru, Pheasants Eye, Purple Mallow, Arbor Judae, Embroiderd Cranes bill,
Dwarf Dutch Tulip, Indian Queen Ranunculus, Yellow Austrian rose, Double white Mountain Ranunculus, Dutch yellow Ranunculus, Indian King Ranunculus, Yellow globe flower, Red Austrian rose,
Cytissus Secundus Clusii, Lotus with yellow flowers,
Virginian Columbine, White Asphodil, Yellow As-
phodil, Princess's Pink.

1 Cinamon Rose.	9 Belsilvia Anemone	18 Arbor Judæ.	26 Yellow globe flower.
2 Narrow-Leav'd Strip'd flow-er de-luce.	10 Venetian Vetch	19 Embrouderd Cranes bill.	27 Red Austrian rose.
3 Columbine Strip'd.	11 Blew Hyacinth of peru.	20 Dwarf Dutch Tulip.	28 Cytisus Secundus Clusii.
4 Bishop of Canterbury Tulip.	12 China pink.	21 Indian Queen Ranunculus.	29 Lotus with yellow flow-ers.
5 Double Catch fly.	13 Savoy Spider wort.	22 Yellow Austrian rose.	
6 Late white Hyacinth.	14 Double Orange Lilly.	23 Double white Mountain Ra-nunculus.	30 Virginian Columbine.
7 Blew-bell Hyacinth	15 White Hyacinth of peru.		31 White Asphodil.
8 Mountain bulbed Crow foot.	16 Pheasants Eye.	24 Dutch yellow Ranunculus.	32 Yellow Asphodil.
	17 Purple Mallow.	25 Indian King Ranunculus.	33 Princess Pink.

MAY

Design'd by P.ˢ Castools.   From the Collection of Rob.ᵗ Furber Gardiner at Kensington. 1730.   Engrav'd by H. Fletcher.

JUNE

Perennial Dwarf Sun flower: Ultramarine & Prusian blew, Iris Major Blue Nigella or Fennel flower, Moon Trefoile, Upright Sweet William, Saxifrage, Cinquefoile, Pansies or Heart-ease, Maidens blush Rose, Yellow Jasmine, Blue Corn flower, Blush Belgick Rose, The Francford Rose, Double Martagon, Orchis or Bee flower, Scarlet Colutea, Fraxinella, Moss province Rose, Double Virginian Silkgrass, White Rose, Dutch Hundred Leav'd Rose, White Batchelors Button, Rosa Mundi, Mountain Lychnis, Dwarf Iris Strip'd, White Jasmine, Scarlet Geranium, Yellow Martagon, Red Martagon, Seucrium or Germander, Mountain dwarf Pink, Yellow Corn Marygold, Purple Sweet Pea, Greek Valerian.

1 Perennial dwarf sun flower.
2 Ultamarine & Prusian blew.
   Iris Major.
3 Blew Nigella,
   or Fennel flower.
4 Moon Trefoile.
5 Upright Sweet William.
6 Saxifrage.
7 Cinque foile.

8 Pansies, or Hearts-ease.
9 Maidens blush Rose.
10 Yellow Jasmine.
11 Blew Corn flower.
12 Blush Belgick Rose.
13 The Franeford Rose.
14 Double Martagon.
15 Orchis or Bee flower.
16 Scarlet Colutea.

JUNE

17 Fraxinella.
18 Moss province Rose.
19 Double Virginian Silk-grass.
20 White Rose.
21 Dutch Hundred Leav'd Rose
22 White Batchelors Button.
23 Rosa Mundi.
24 Mountain Lychnis.
25 Dwarf Iris Strip'd.

26 White Jasmine.
27 Scarlet Geranium.
28 Yellow Martagon.
29 Red Martagon.
30 Teucrium or Germander.
31 Mountain dwarf Pink.
32 Yellow Corn Marygold.
33 Purple sweet Pea.
34 Greek Valerian.

Design'd by P.r Casteel

From the Collection of Rob.t Furber, Gardiner at Kensington. 1730.

Engrav'd by H. Fletcher.

107

JULY

Double Nasturtium, Double white Maudlin, Prince
picoté July flower, True Caper, Virginian yellow
Jasmine, Painted Lady Carnation, Double blew
Throat-wort, Scarlet Martagon, White Lilly strip'd
with purple, Spanish Broom, Carolina kidney bean
tree, Double strip'd female balsom, True Olive tree,
Red Oleander, Painted Lady pink, White Lupin,
Princess picoté July flower, Geranium noctu olens,
White Valerian, Hop Horn beam, Indian or china
pink, Double Pomegranate, Double mouse ear, Vir-
ginian Scarlet honey suckle, Double white Throat-
wort, French Marigold, Double scarlet Lychnis,
Double blew Larkspur, Hungarian Climer, Double
Stock, Bean Caper, White Oleander.

1 Double Nasturtium.
2 Double white Maudlin.
3 Prince picote July flower.
4 True Caper.
5 Virginian yellow Jasmine.
6 Painted Lady Carnation.
7 Double blew Throat-wort.
8 Scarlet Martagon.
9 White Lilly strip'd with purple.
10 Spanish Broom.
11 Carolina kidney bean tree.
12 Double strip'd female balsom.
13 True Olive tree.
14 Red Oleander.
15 Painted Lady pink.
16 White Lupin.

JULY

17 Princess picote July flower.
18 Geranium noctu olens.
19 White Valerian.
20 Hop Horn beam.
21 Indian or china pink.
22 Double Pomegranate.
23 Double mouse ear.
24 Virginian Scarlet honey suckle.
25 Double white Throat-wort.
26 French Marigold.
27 Double scarlet Lychnis.
28 Double blew Larkspur.
29 Hungarian Climer.
30 Double Stock.
31 Bean Caper.
32 White Oleander.

Design'd by P.r Cass'teels.   From the Collection of Rob.t Furber Gardner at Kensington. 1730.   Engrav'd by H. Fletcher

109

AUGUST

Purple Althaea frutex, Ivy leav'd Jasmine, Iris
Uvaria, Purple Sultan, Purple toad flax, Purple
Amaranthoides, Double Arabian Jasmine, Yellow
Kelmia, Purple Coxcomb Amaranth, Shrub St.
Johns wort, Pona's blew Throat-wort, Palma
Christi, Purple Convolvulus, Polyanthos, Indian yel-
low Jasmine, Double flowering Myrtle, Egyptian
scarlet holly hock, Yellow strip'd marvel of peru,
Strip'd Monthly rose, double fether few, Semper
Augustus Auricula, Dwarf Convolvulus, Willow
leav'd Apocynum, Apios of America, Virginian
flowering Raspberry, Zisole from Genoa, Double
spanish Jasmine, White Eternal, Fruit bearing Passion flower, Scarlet Althaea, Canary shrub fox
glove, Long blowing honey suckle, Double purple
Virgins bower, Virginian scarlet Martagon.

1 Purple Althæa frutex.	9 Purple Coxcomb Amaranth.	17 Egyptian scarlet holly hock.	26 Lisole from Genoa.
2 Ivy leav'd Jasmine.	10 Shrub St. Johns wort.	18 Yellow strip'd marvel of peru.	27 Double spanish Jasmine.
3 Iris Uvaria.	11 Pona's blew Throatwort.	19 Strip'd Monthly rose.	28 White Eternal.
4 Purple Sultan.	12 Palma Christi.	20 Double, fether few.	29 Fruit bearing Passion flower.
5 Purple toad flax.	13 Purple Convolvulus.	21 Semper Augustus Auricula.	30 Scarlet Althæa.
6 Purple Amaranthoides.	14 Polyanthos.	22 Dwarf Convolvulus.	31 Canary shrub fox glove.
7 Double Arabian Jasmine.	15 Indian yellow Jasmine.	23 Willow leav'd Apocynum.	32 Long blowing honey suckle.
8 Yellow Retinia.	16 Double flowering Myrtle.	24 Apios of America.	33 Double purple Virgins bower.
		25 Virginian flowering Raspberry.	34 Virginian scarlet Martagon.

AUGUST

Design'd by P.ᵗ Casteels.   From the Collection of Robᵗ Furber Gardiner at Kensington 1730.   Engrav'd by H. Fletcher.

111

SEPTEMBER

Red Sow Bread, White Sow Bread, White Corn-marigold, New Tree Primrose, Sour leav'd Geranium, Quill'd African Marigold, Hearts ease, Shrub Cotton, Sheffords Hester Auricula, Virginian Birth-wort, Virginian upright Bramble, Scarlet Indian Cane, White Colchicum, Bean Caper, All red Amaranthus, Double white Soapwort, Yellow Indian Cane, Virginian Poke, Gentianella, White monthly Rose, Yellow Amaranthus, Oriental Arssmart, Broad leav'd Cardinal, Yellow Colchicum, Hardy golden Rod, White Althaea frutex, Chequer'd Colchicum, Yellow Colutea, Dwarf Pomgranate, Strip'd single Female balsom, African Marigold, Honour & glory Auricula, White flower Moth Mullein, Double Colchicum, Three leaved Passion flower.

113

OCTOBER

Tuberose flower, Single Nasturtium, Yellow peren.
[perennial] Poppy, Purple Polyanthos, Saffron
flower, Strip'd double Colchicum, Single blew Periwinkle, Trump flower, Camomile double, Semper
Augustus Auricula, Indian Tobacco, Arbutus double, Best flowering Geranium, Guernsey Lilly, Autumn Carnation, Agnus Castus, Long blowing
Honey suckle, Spiked Aster, Belladona Lilly, Ever
green Honey suckle, Leonurus or Archangel tree,
Black Cranes bill, Scarlet Cranes bill, Marigold tree,
Musk Scabious, Double white Musk rose, Box
leav'd Myrtle, Michaelmas Daisie, Yellow Passion
flower, Holly-hock always double, Virginian Shrub
Acre.

1	Tuberose flower.	9	Camomile double.	17	Long blowing Honeysuckle.
2	Single Nasturtium.	10	Semper Augustus Auricula.	18	Spiked Aster.
3	Yellow peren.ll Poppy.	11	Indian Tobacco.	19	Belladona Lilly.
4	Purple Polyanthos.	12	Arbutus double.	20	Ever green Honeysuckle.
5	Saffron flower.	13	Best flowering Geranium.	21	Leonurus, or Archangel tree.
6	Strip'd double Colchicum.	14	Guernsey Lilly.	22	Black Cranes bill.
7	Single blew Perivinkle.	15	Autumn Carnation.	23	Scarlet Cranes bill.
8	Trumpet flower.	16	Agnus Castus.	24	Marigold tree.

OCTOBER

25	Musk Scabious.
26	Double white Musk rose.
27	Box leav'd Myrtle.
28	Michaelmas Daisie.
29	Yellow Passion flower.
30	Hollyhock always double.
31	Virgina Shrub Acre.

Design'd by L.ct Casteels.

From the Collection of Rob.t Furber Gardiner at Kensington. 1730.

Engrav'd by H. Fletcher.

115

NOVEMBER

Ficoides or fig Marigold, White Periwinkle, Earliest
flowering Laurustinus, Blew Periwinkle, Tree Candy
tuft, Embroider'd Cranes bill, Yellow spik'd Eternal, Strip'd single Anemone, Borage, Thyme leav'd
Myrtle, French Marigold, Colchicum, Agripina
major, Ilex leav'd Jasmines, Great purple Cranes
bill, Arbutus or Strawberry tree, Double Nasturtium,
Broad leav'd red Valerian, Myrto Cistus, Virginian
Aster, Campanula Canariensis Pheasants Eye, Perennial dwarf Sun flower, Double Featherfew, Carolina Star flower, Scarlet Althaea, Spanish white
Jasmine, Lavender with divided Leaves, Golden
Rod, American Viburnum, Yellow Dwarf Aloe,
Single blew Anemone, Purple Ficoides, Groundsell
tree, Pellitory with Daisy flowers, Scarlet single
anemone, White Egyptian holly-hock, Caper Bush,
Dwarf Colutea.

1 Ficoides or fig Marigold.	11 French Marigold.	21 Pheasants Eye.	30 Yellow Dwarf Aloe.
2 White Periwinkle.	12 Colchicum Agrypina major.	22 Perennial dwarf Sun flower.	31 Single blew Anemone.
3 Earliest flowering Laurustinus.	13 Ilex leav'd Ismines.	23 Double Feather few.	32 Purple Ficoides.
4 Blew Periwinkle.	14 Great purple Cranes bill.	24 Carolina Star flower.	33 Groundsell tree.
5 Tree Candy tuft.	15 Arbutus or Straw berry tree.	25 Scarlet Althæa.	34 Pellitory with Daisy flower.
6 Embroider'd Cranes bill.	16 Double Nasturtium.	26 Spanish white Jasmine.	35 Scarlet single Anemone.
7 Yellow spik'd Eternal.	17 Broad leav'd red Valerian.	27 Lavender with divided Leaves.	36 White Egyptian holly hock.
8 Strip'd single Anemone.	18 Myrtle Cistus.	28 Golden Rod.	37 Caper Bush.
9 Borage.	19 Virginian Aster.	29 American Viburnum.	38 Dwarf Colutea.
10 Thyme leav'd Myrtle.	20 Campanula Canariensis.		

NOVEMBER

Design'd by P.r Casteels.   From the Collection of Rob.t Furber Gardiner at Kensington. 1730.   Engrav'd by H. Fletcher.

117

DECEMBER

Royal purple Auricula, African white flower'd
Heath, Pansies or Hearts ease, White Corn Mari-
gold, Strawberry daisie, Cape Marigold, Shining
leav'd Laurustinus, Marvel du Monde Auricula,
Red spring Cyclamen, White Cyclamen, Yellow
Ficoides, Yellow round Eternal, Christmas flower,
Winter white Primrose, Gentianella, Yellow Corn
Marigold, Scarlet Geranium, Canary Pellitory, Va-
lerianella, Winter double Crowfoot, Strip'd leav'd
Geranium, Cape Marigold white within, St. Peters
Shrub, Mountain Avens, Single purple Anemone,
Sage & Rosemary tree, Winter wall flower, Winter
flowering Pear, Lavender-leav'd Groundsel tree,
Scarlet African Aloe with Pineapple Leaves, Span-
ish Virgins bower, Glastenbury thorne, Humble
plant, Basella, Monthly rose bud, Trifid African
golden knob.

1 Royal purple Auricula.	10 White Cyclamen.		19 Valerianella.	28 Winter flowering Pear.
2 African white flower'd Heath.	11 Yellow Ficoides.		20 Winter double Crowfoot.	29 Lavender leav'd Groundsel tree.
3 Pansies or Hearts ease.	12 Yellow round Eternal.		21 Strip'd leav'd Geranium.	30 Scarlet African Aloe, with Pineapple Leaves.
4 White Corn Marigold.	13 Christmas flower.		22 Cape Marigold white within	
5 Strawberry daisie.	14 Winter white Primrose.		23 S.t Peters Shrub.	31 Spanish Virgins bower.
6 Cape Marigold.	15 Gentianella.		24 Mountain Avens.	32 Glastenbury thorne.
7 Shining leav'd Laurustinus.	16 Yellow Corn Marigold.		25 Single purple Anemone.	33 Humble plant.
8 Marvel du Monde Auricula.	17 Scarlet Geranium.		26 Sage & Rosemary tree.	34 Basella.
9 Red spring Cyclamen.	18 Canary Pellitory.*		27 Winter wall flower.	35 Monthly rose bud.
		DECEMBER		36 Trifid African golden knot.

Design'd by J.no Casteels.   From the Collection of Rob.t Furber gardiner at Kensington. 1730.   Engrav'd by H. Fletcher.

119

V

...AND MAN INVENTED FLOWERS

by R. Milton Carleton

ONLY those who have reached maturity—whether a maturity of time or of judgment—can fully understand progress. Although the privilege of creating and promulgating the new falls largely upon those young in years, to appreciate what has been accomplished demands perspective and knowledge of the past.

This is as true of horticulture as it is of the atomic age. Not until one sits down to consider gardening in retrospect can the true significance of the revolution that has taken place in the past two decades be brought into perspective. The word "revolution" rather than "evolution" is used here, in full awareness of its true meaning. For what has happened all around us, catching us unaware, is an upheaval unprecedented in garden history.

In the past two decades more progress has been made in the control of every phase of plant culture than was made in all the previous recorded history of horticulture. This revolution we* are witnessing falls naturally under

* The Editor has asked me to define the editorial We. Unfortunately, living as I do a triple life, I find this difficult. First, perhaps I am speaking of the thousands of amateur gardeners I know (among whom I number myself) who love plants and try to understand them. Second, I cannot ignore the fact that I earn my living in a commercial establishment connected with seeds and plants. Third, I cannot omit from that all-encompassing We the hundreds of plant scientists with whom I have worked and consulted.

122

two general headings. First, the scientific control of plant growth has given us the means for manipulating that growth to our own ends. Each separate discovery (whether it be that of hormones to stimulate roots, maleic hydrazide, to throw growth into low gear, or some other aspect of juggling plant physiology), is but a part of the larger pattern of control—the manipulation of natural phenomena to our own ends.

This vast program of control over the environment of the plant is considered elsewhere, in Chapter VII.

Coequal with our new skills in growth regulation is the new science of plant breeding. In many ways the progress in this field is even more amazing than that which results from our control of the external environment of plants, for here we are dealing with forces all but unknown a few decades ago.

As everyone who has opened an old rose catalogue after the passage of twenty years or so knows, most of the varieties described then as the best of their class have completely disappeared from commerce. Today they are found only in the collections of those who treasure them nostalgically.

What often escapes us, however, is that the rose of today—as typified by the variety Peace—simply did not exist until man deliberately created it. When he wants increased size, he can also treat the parent plants with colchicine, to force a change in the reproductive cells and the resulting progeny. If two parent plants refuse to cross, he tries chemical stimulants to make the foreign pollen acceptable to the female parent. Thus the rose of today is largely man-made— the product of man's control over nature.

To appreciate how revolutionary this is, think back to the time when we considered plants all but immutable. What variations did occur were attributed to chance—to forces beyond the control of man. Contrast that with our ability to produce plants that are taller, healthier, more floriferous, by altering the inner structure of the cell, and then controlling the environment in which this superplant is grown.

We cannot, however, credit all this amazing development to the breeder of ornamental plants. Without the incentive of profit, which brought into being hybrid corn—the greatest single achievement in plant science—we would have been a long time developing the modern man-made plant, whether it be a rose, a petunia, or a cabbage. Although the epic of hybrid corn has been completely explained before this, let us borrow a leaf, as it were, from the corn breeder's book to give us an understanding of the less widely publicized breeding of ornamentals.

Hybrid corn is the product of using the inherited tendencies of plants to change minutely from generation to generation. Such changes are caused by the fact that in nature no two plants are identical in every trait, though outwardly the same. Through the years these variations tend to cancel each other, so that a wild species reaches a natural balance.* Only when conditions occur that bring about changes that increase survival value of the species do they persist long enough to become evident. Even such changes usually take place so slowly that they are not visible except over periods longer than a single lifetime.† Out of these rare circumstances come the occasional species or subspecies that arise, apparently spontaneously, in nature.

The hybrid-corn breeder uses the fact that plants are both male and female to produce these changes in a much shorter time. Since a plant can be bred to itself by excluding foreign male elements (flying pollen) and using its own pollen to fertilize its own silks, highly uniform plants can be produced. These are further inbred for several generations, thus fixing the desirable qualities for which they were selected.

The same type of breeding is being done meanwhile with other plants differing considerably in their characteristics. When two such inbred lines are then crossed, each transmits the desirable traits that dominate in it. This concentration of good qualities results in a plant that excels either parent in the factors for which they were inbred.

In addition to this intensifying of desirable traits a second result takes place. No scientist has ever given a satisfactory explanation of this, though it is well known, and is possible to produce empirically through hybrid breeding. The seedlings from such a cross have what is known as heterosis or hybrid vigor. They are taller, bigger in all parts, and more resistant to disease than either parent.

It is because of heterosis that hybrid plants have become so popular.

Although the breeding of ornamentals along similar lines has resulted in the amazing new flowers we enjoy today, this development did not take place immediately. Vegetable breeders, aware of the commercial advantages of earlier maturity, greater production, and increased size, were the first to utilize these techniques. It has been only within the past five years that true inbred hybrids of flowers, produced in the same way as hybrid corn, have made their appearance in general commerce.

The knowledgeable gardener will at once recall that we have always had "hybrids" in flower seed. Usually of European origin, these were mixtures that displayed a wide range of colors, larger flowers, or superior vigor. How, then, do modern hybrids differ from these mixtures?

---

* One fact that must be considered is that in plants survival of the species in a highly competitive natural state is the major motivating force. When Man uses plants, the need for seed survival, for toughness, and for other qualities that make survival possible is largely eliminated. Hence the plant scientist often works to enhance qualities that would mean the destruction of the plant if it were compelled to struggle in its natural environment.

† Since breeding is being discussed, the familiar sports that arise spontaneously are not considered here.

124

The older mixtures were usually crosses between flowers that differed widely in color or habit. The idea behind their production was to get greater variation in the seedlings. In hybrid corn the variation is concentrated in the parent lines, so that the offspring will exhibit only the best of the parent qualities, with as little variation as possible. As confusing as this seems, we now recognize two (possibly three) kinds of hybrids today.

To distinguish between them, many scientists call modern varieties of this type F_1 hybrids. The F_1 stands for "first filial generation," or the first generation from seed. However, since the offspring of *any* cross, whether produced by modern breeding or not, is a first filial generation, I feel the words "inbred hybrid" more accurately describe the modern product.

One of the important advantages of such inbred hybrids is their earlier maturity. All the true inbred hybrids I have tested will emerge from the soil at least one third faster than will comparable non-hybrid varieties. Whenever I am testing new varieties designated as hybrids, I watch the seedling stage. If they are late in emerging as compared with known inbred hybrids, I know the label has been applied to them without justification in hopes of increasing sales.

This earlier start is followed by earlier maturity, an advantage that is held right up to flowering time. For example, in testing the new hybrid Indian Series of small-flowered petunias in the spring of 1954, these were in flower exactly nine days before non-hybrid sorts opened their first buds. The hybrid Paleface was the first of all petunias to bloom and held that advantage right up to frost.

In the past early flowering was associated with early decline, so that early varieties were expected to quit blooming before the later sorts. This has not proved true in the case of inbred hybrids, which continue to flower longer than do non-hybrids.

Although this advantage alone would justify the use of inbred hybrids, it has been extended one step further through the breeder's skill. In 1956 seedsmen will be due for an introduction to inbred petunia hybrids that are also male-sterile. This male sterility will occur only in the generation grown by the home gardener.

At first sight this does not seem like much of an advantage until we remember that annual flowers usually slow up in flowering once they have set seed. Some annuals stop flowering as soon as the first seeds are set. Another important effect of pollination is that the flower, having fulfilled its destiny, starts to fade.

For this reason a plant that does not produce fertile pollen has tremendous advantages. Since the blossoms are not pollinated, no seed is produced and the plant stays in bloom until cut down by frost. The individual blooms, deprived of the chance for pollination, keep fresh and unfaded until the stem attaching them to the plant shrivels. I have marked individual flowers on these plants and have seen them as fresh on the third week as the day they opened.

Another example of the revolution in plants has already been mentioned—the obsolescence of the roses of yesterday. Upon opening the 1932 catalogue of a world-famous rose firm I was struck by the fact that of the thirty novelties offered during that year only two—Autumn and Mrs. Pierre du Pont —are commonly planted today, and even these are represented by better modern varieties.

Rose breeding has made progress at a breathless pace, not only in America, but in Germany and France. What is significant is that this is largely *planned* progress, the result of using the techniques of science to produce deliberately new roses to meet specific demands. Modern roses are man-made, and not the result of haphazard crossing of varieties that might be good parents, but more likely will prove otherwise.

Although planned, this does not mean that progress can be made over night. An excellent example of this is that relatively new class—the Flori-bundas. The first of these appeared about twenty-five years ago, the result of crossing old-fashioned polyanthas from Europe with hybrid tea roses by American breeders. Each year has seen more progress made, but it was not until the past five years that the lessons learned from hybrid corn breeders have been used to produce made-to-order colors in Floribundas; new roses in all imaginable colors will soon be available in this class. Plant habit has been improved, vigor increased, and floriferousness leaves little to be desired.

Progress in breeding along these lines is ever-expanding. Once a line is fixed, it becomes a potential parent. Thus the breeder finds himself with more good things than he can profitably introduce at times.

Fashion, perhaps one of the great roses of all times, must be counted as the most important Floribunda of the past five years. Without the use of modern breeding techniques its unusual peach-salmon-apricot color might never have been obtained. Its stablemate, Pinocchio, cannot be considered as the product of the past five years, but deserves mention here because of its pre-potency. Already the parent of several splendid new varieties, its influence will be seen more and more in varieties still to be introduced. The Pinocchio family, whose latest member, Jiminy Cricket, is the All-America Rose Selection of 1955, will live long in rose history.

Unfortunately for our purpose, an evaluation of the best plants of the past few years, in the previous decade two roses were introduced that were so important and so significant that none since has matched them. Peace, from France, which many consider the greatest rose of all time, will make tough competition for any rose subsequently introduced. Although Peace is not my favorite rose, I acknowledge its greatness. Another really magnificent rose, also the product of man's skill in juggling the elements of inheritance, is Charlotte Armstrong, which for me has a charm Peace never will have.

That Peace and Charlotte Armstrong will have competition is inevitable. I have observed Tiffany, the All-America Hybrid Tea selection for 1955 in several gardens. Everywhere it showed signs of being a seedling of Charlotte Armstrong, with a more delicate coloring. If it continues to improve, as most roses do the second year after planting, it could give its parent stiff competition.

The years ahead should certainly be of tremendous interest to rose lovers.

ANNUALS Petunias, already mentioned as examples of hybrid vigor, have made greater progress than other ornamental inbred hybrids. The first inbred hybrid ornamental that could be grown by the home gardener was a petunia—Silver Medal. The impact of this variety was tremendous. Less than two years after its introduction it had made obsolete all other pink bedding varieties, and was being planted by practically every progressive grower of bedding plants.

Silver Medal is an inbred hybrid between the large-flowered single type, notoriously difficult for the amateur to grow, and the small-flowered bedding type. Despite its large-flowered ancestry it has proved easy for the amateur to germinate because of its hybrid vigor.

Unfortunately, in spite of these good qualities, Silver Medal shows its hybrid origin by growing too tall, owing to a lack of care in selecting the parent lines from which it was produced. It is almost impossible to keep down to less than fifteen inches, far too tall for a bedding petunia.

In 1953, however, a new petunia of the same type of breeding, but from parents selected for dwarf habit, was introduced. This cross resulted in a new variety named Linda, which promises to become the number-one bedding plant among annuals. It duplicates the salmon-pink color of Silver Medal, in a somewhat richer shade on a plant that never exceeds 10 inches in height, expressing its hybrid vigor by spreading to a width of 36 inches.

The progress possible through the use of inbred techniques is well illustrated by the brilliant red petunia Comanche. Its clear Indian-red flowers are extremely uniform in color and the plants are uniform in height. Overnight it made obsolete its non-hybrid parent, Fire Chief. This is all the more remarkable when it is realized that Fire Chief won the All-America Award in 1950 as the best annual of that year. In 1953, just three short years later, it was superseded by its hybrid descendant.

Perhaps the most difficult of all hybrids to produce is the all-double

127

strain of petunia. The breeding behind them is complex, since only single flowers will set seed, hence one parent must be a single, yet produce a double offspring.

Their production was a closely held Japanese secret. American breeders had no parent lines that would produce only double flowers from a single-double cross.

During the war, however, American breeders, with Japanese imports cut off, went to work to break down the parent lines. After long, patient breeding and selection they not only found parents that would breed as expected, but these were actually improvements on their Japanese parents. Today Japanese double petunias are considered much inferior to the All Double Pan American Strain.

The variety Sonata, a huge white snowball with fringed, fully double flowers, is by far the best of these. It is almost matched in beauty by Nocturne, a rich, deep purple of the same formation. Both of these must be included in any list of the best annuals of the past five years.

Marigolds, difficult to handle as hybrids because of their flower formation, have been produced as pure-line parents, but are not sold as such. These inbred lines were used to produce a cross previously considered almost impossible—between the tall-African type and the dwarf-French class. The finest of these crosses, called Parisian hybrids, has the greatest color range found in marigolds. The flowers are produced in both solids and mixtures of colors. These range from pure lemon yellow to deep maroon, with every possible variation and combination in blotched, mottled, and striped contrasting colors.

Another variety produced by hybrid techniques, although not offered as such, is the 1953 All-America winner, Alyssum Royal Carpet. Selections of the older Violet Queen, beautiful in color but too tall in habit, were inbred to intensify the natural compact habit of the selected plants. Once fixed, seed from these lines could then be produced without further use of hybrid methods.

The same use of hybrid breeding to produce original parent stocks was followed in the development of what promises to be one of the great annuals of all times—the All-America winner for 1954—Zinnia Blaze. A well-grown planting of Blaze must be seen to be believed. Here is one of those singing, vibrant colors so rare in flowers—a brilliant tangerine scarlet that dominates any garden in which it is planted. The individual blooms are more than 5 inches across, of an interesting, quilled formation that classifies Blaze as a cactus-flowered variety.

The reason why Blaze, as well as other cactus-flowered zinnias, and Parisian-hybrid marigold cannot be produced for sale as true inbred hybrids is interesting. The high-school student of botany will recognize them as Compositae, flowers with composite heads made up of hundreds of individual florets inside a single bloom. To produce true inbred hybrids, each of these individual flowers would have to be emasculated by hand, removing the pollen-producing stamens, so the flower would not set seed with its own pollen. If this is not done, no hybrid would result.

Obviously this would require a tremendous amount of labor. Unless the seed could be sold at a fabulous price, first-generation seed would be out of the question. Thus, although true hybrids in the wider sense of the word, these are not real inbred hybrids like the other new flowers already described. The seed you buy is several generations removed from the hybrid parents.

Although introduced several years ago, the Cuthbertson hot-weather sweet peas have only been appreciated during the past three or four years. Because of their ability to flower during summer heat, even in the Middle West, this outstanding strain has brought back the sweet pea as a garden flower where they have not been grown for years. Sales by dealers have practically doubled each year during the last four seasons, indicating a growing appreciation of their worth.

They have as rivals for honors another strain of sweet peas, not particularly noted for heat resistance, but of superior size and freedom of bloom. The new Zvolenak Multiflora strain produces five to six individual blooms on a single stem, in contrast to three or four smaller flowers produced by ordinary varieties. This gain in the number of flowers is offset by the fact that the spaces between the blooms is much wider than ordinary. When cut for use in bouquets, this is not noticeable, and the stems make a magnificent show. This strain is of great importance as the possible ancestor of a new race of sweet peas that will combine the qualities of the Cuthbertson strain with the more spectacular bloom of the Zvolenak hybrid.

Last spring, when I visited the California flower-seed producers, practically every workshop plot had some experimental crosses developed toward this end.

PERENNIALS   Progress is slower than with the more readily propagated annuals. Each generation requires from two to four years, and as many as eight generations may be needed to fix some elusive quality. Add to that the fact that the demand for seed of even the finest perennials is only a fraction of the demand for those of annuals, and it is obvious why few new perennials appear in commerce.

It is not surprising, therefore, that an amateur (who does not count the cost of all the basic breeding necessary) is the breeder of the outstanding new hybrid perennial of 1955. The McKana strain of Aquilegia represents several decades of careful selection and inbreeding to produce the unusual range of colors it includes.

The tremendous flowers of this strain must be seen to be believed. I have measured them fully 5 inches across, with spurs in proportion. The strain includes both the brilliant, clear colors of the Dobbie's hybrids and the Scott Elliott pastel tints.

Everyone who grows perennials must of necessity know the magnificent Pacific hybrid delphiniums. On the West Coast these act like true perennials but have been less permanent in the Middle West and East. If grown as biennials in these sections, with a one-year-old crop coming along each year to give continuous bloom, these are without question the most satisfactory blue flowers we have for the permanent border.

Although the blue and white colors have been in commerce for years, only within the past three years has a really new color been added to this strain. Called Astolat, this is the first near-pink delphinium of quality to be offered by anyone.

This is not a plant to be grown without selection. The color factors for pink are so hard to fix that Astolat will vary considerably in color. Some of these are lovely, particularly the soft flesh and shell pinks. Some of the dull-plum pinks and mulberry magentas are nothing short of ugly. By seeding early, so a short spike can be produced the first year, and discarding all that are not attractive, the gardener can check the colors in the seedbed. The better pink spikes are nothing short of sensational when contrasted with the white, lavender, and blue spikes of the other Pacific varieties.

WOODY PLANTS Until recently there has been little or no interest in breeding shrubs. At least 95 per cent of the new shrubs that came into commerce were the result of accidental variations from seed, not deliberate breeding for new types.

What is not commonly appreciated, however, is that the nursery industry has recently gone through a violent revolution. Suddenly nurserymen everywhere find as much as 75 per cent of their inventory obsolete. Stocks of what were once bread-and-butter items like spirea Van Houttei, privet, honeysuckle, and tall cotoneasters have suddenly gone completely out of favor.

The reason for this loss of demand is the popularity of the one-story house. Whether it is called a ranch house, rambler, spreader, or what not, the modern low, one-story home has made useless much of what the old-line landscape architect learned during his school years.

He was taught to plant foundations, to hide the break between the foundation and the house, and to tie the structure to the ground. Here is a style that is already so close to the ground that it needs no further "pulling down." He has been taught about vistas and the need for a central axis, with vertical interest at the far end of the axis. The modern small house is probably built on the

130

largest lot the owner can afford, with no room for such elaborate treatment. The picture window, hardly a foot above the ground, cannot be planted with old-style shrubs without hiding it completely.

As can be imagined, this revolution has made nurserymen sit up and take notice. Every type of dwarf plant has been examined carefully and the scramble for new material is lively. For the past four years *Ribes alpinum,* the Alpine currant, has been practically unobtainable: once the only commonly available dwarf hedging plant, it has been planted at a rate that may bring it into the same disrepute with better gardeners that privet suffers under today.

An indication of what demand will be in the future is a new barberry from Holland, introduced for the first time in 1952—Berberis Crimson Pygmy. The plants grow about eight inches tall with a spread of from 15 to 18 inches. In habit it is the perfect plant for that "turning corner" where the drive and side-walk meet, to keep visitors from cutting across the lawn. It is high enough to present a mental obstacle to such short cuts.

The color of the old foliage is a deep, bronzy red. The new growth is a bright rose-red, glowing in full sun. It is so attractive and useful that we can only hope Crimson Pygmy is the forerunner of a whole race of low-growing shrubs for landscaping ranch homes.

Although not quite as dwarfed, another lovely woody plant is the Hypericum Hidcote variety, from the well-known Hidcote estate in England, now the property of the British nation. In the United States, north of the Ohio River, this is often frozen to the ground, but blooms on new wood produced the following spring. This new growth stands about 2 feet high. South of the Ohio it can be expected to survive as a woody shrub, reaching a final height of 3 to 4 feet.

The bright yellow cup-shaped blooms are about 2 inches across, produced freely from July until frost. It is a lovely thing to plant below a picture window, or at either side of the front door of a ranch home.

Another new shrub, one that reaches a final height of as much as seven feet, is *Viburnum carlcephalum.* Although a lovely thing, it will probably remain unknown until someone gives it a more usable name. This is a hybrid of the well-known *Viburnum carlesi* and the less-known *Viburnum macrocephalum.*

Its flowers, big balls of white tinted with pink, are intensely fragrant. It is slightly later than *Viburnum carlesi* in season. Its most important advantage over its parent variety is the brilliant autumn coloring of the leaves.

HYBRID TREES The homeowner who lives where the American elm is the dominant street species has given thought to the need for new trees. Here is a species threatened with extinction by two virulent diseases—phloem necrosis and Dutch elm disease. He thinks immediately of the possibilities of breeding resistant species. A good deal of work has been started with this idea in mind.

Unfortunately tree breeding is not for the man in a hurry. If started today, the chances are that most of us will be beyond appreciating trees when the first results of the work are introduced into general commerce. I know of hybrid trees that were seedlings twenty to thirty years ago that still have not been released for sale. Most of them are held up for lack of practical methods of propagating them without losing the advantages of hybrid vigor.

Obviously this is work that belongs properly to government agencies, not in the commercial establishment that could go bankrupt trying to finance tree breeding.

This leaves only the selection of chance seedlings of superior quality as our hope for new trees in the near future. That this need not be a case of Hobson's choice can be judged from the Moraine locust, the finest new tree to be introduced in the past quarter century. A chance seedling isolated from a block of saplings of the thornless honey locust, it comes close to matching the specifications for a perfect shade tree. Best of all, in form it so closely resembles the American elm that it can be interplanted with existing rows of elms without destroying their arching grace. The foliage, light and feathery, is not unlike that of the elm when viewed from below.

It is a male tree, which means that it will not produce the unsightly pods that make the ordinary honey locust so undesirable. In this respect it is even cleaner than the American elm, which seeds so copiously in May and June.

The honey locust (and its variety, the Moraine locust) is not attacked by any serious disease or insect pest. The one possible threat is the stem borer, which I saw attacking this species in Denver, but I know of no other area where it does so.

NEW GRASSES Perhaps the most exciting developments in new plants are the introductions of new grasses by the U. S. Department of Agriculture. For the first time in history we actually have at our command grasses that originated within the United States, in areas where summer temperatures are unfavorable to European species.

This solves one of the major problems confronting the homeowner, who until now has had to use alien species. We now realize that of the species commonly used for lawns not one originated in the United States. Even the well-known Kentucky bluegrass came to Kentucky via England, where it grows continually all summer long in the relatively low temperatures found there. In Kentucky, as well as over most of the United States, it becomes dormant with the arrival of high summer temperatures, which allows weeds to invade the lawn.

132

The newest hybrid grass is Meyer zoysia, a man-made species from the world's greatest plant experiment station at Beltsville, Maryland. It is a hybrid between Zoysia matrella and Zoysia japonica. It combines the high resistance to cold and drought of the latter species with the finer leaf of the less hardy Zoysia matrella.

The resultant hybrid is perhaps the most perfectly adapted lawn grass in existence within its natural range. No known insect or disease can attack it. It seems to thrive on drought: I have seen it lush and green during a spell when less than 2 inches of rain fell from May to September, and when the thermometer soared above one hundred day after day. In the Washington, D.C., area it remains in active growth from May to September.

It tolerates low mowing: lawn experts recommend cutting it to a height of ½ inch.

So vigorously does it grow under adverse conditions that weeds cannot become established in it. The only lawn species that seems to be able to compete with it is Merion bluegrass, and this only over a relatively limited range.

Although it richly deserves the name of a wonder grass, Meyer zoysia is not without its faults. For one thing, it turns brown with the first frost. What is more, it stays brown until air temperatures go well above 80° in spring. North of a line drawn from Kansas City to New York City it does not really green up until nearly June. When it is dormant, it is the deadest brown imaginable—the color of a coco door mat.

For this reason pure stands of Meyer zoysia belong south of the Ohio River, in areas where other lawn grasses do not thrive. Here the dormant period is shorter and the need for good grasses greater. For a distance of approximately one hundred miles north of this area there is a region where Meyer zoysia may be of value in a mixed lawn, combined with Merion bluegrass. The Merion grows rapidly in spring and fall, so that the dead grass color of Meyer zoysia is partially masked. The combination has most of the good qualities of a pure zoysia turf with better color.

North of this region another new grass has won wider acceptance than any other lawn species ever introduced. Although it has been on the market for only four short years, Merion bluegrass is today accepted as the standard of excellence for all lawns that receive four hours or more of sunshine during the day.

Merion is not a man-made hybrid. It was discovered growing in a Kentucky bluegrass turf near Philadelphia. Although it exhibits all the signs of being a natural hybrid, there are technical reasons why this is said to be impossible. Whatever may be its origin, it exhibits all the vigor of a true inbred hybrid.

Propagated and distributed for testing by the U.S.D.A., it has proved the most widely adapted lawn grass we have for what was once considered natural bluegrass country. Although slow to establish itself from seed, once it gets its roots down and begins to stool out, it forms such a dense turf that even crab grass cannot invade it. It remains bright green and in active growth at all times of the year that the thermometer does not go below freezing. In my own lawn I have seen it turn bright green during thaws in midwinter. It is highly resistant to turf diseases, and is not killed during seasons when bents and fescues are destroyed by leaf spot.

THE FUTURE The use of modern techniques for producing new plants has hardly started. All over the nation breeders are working at top speed to produce new plants, better adapted to their environment, and with new beauty and usefulness. Much of this work cannot be discussed now.

One exception is the new series of lilies now being tested and propagated for introduction by the Bureau of Plant Industry of the U.S.D.A. The most sensational of these are crosses between *Lilium auratum* and *Lilium speciosum*. Imagine the big brilliant gold-and-white flowers of *Lilium auratum* superimposed on the luscious rosy crimson of *Lilium speciosum*. The flowers of these hybrids are huge, even larger than those of *Lilium auratum*. They are rich brocades of crimson, gold, and white, with the bright golden stripe down the center of the petal. Although they vary in the way the color is distributed in the tremendous flowers, all are magnificent.

Now being propagated for general distribution, these should be on the market in five or six years. Watch for them: they will add a new dimension to the genus Lilium. Also watch for the introduction of the new azaleas and camellias now being developed by the U.S.D.A.

VI

GARDENS OF AMERICA

by Marjorie P. Johnson

PHOTOGRAPHY BY GOTTSCHO-SCHLEISNER

THERE are gardens in America today from one coast to the other, from the North to the South and up into our last frontier, Alaska. Yet back in our early days gardens reached perfection mostly in the colonies along the middle Atlantic seaboard. Most of these colonial gardens were formal in the best sense.

Opposite, a restored garden in Colonial Williamsburg. It is simple in design, well balanced, and secluded. The paths are paved with brick (another characteristic of early American gardening), and trees, shrubs, and vines have all been used lovingly and to good purpose. Particularly in the colonial South was there recognition of one of the main functions of the formal garden: to relate the garden area to the architecture of the house.

In America today one of the best places to see examples of parterre gardening is Colonial Williamsburg. At left is such a garden, of formal beds edged with shrubs that can be kept precise and low-growing by clipping.

Still formal, but with its severity softened by the curves of the wrought-iron gateway and informal edgings, is the entrance to the path above, also at Williamsburg.

A present-day version of formal gardening in which flowering trees (dogwoods) and various conifers are contrasted to clipped evergreen hedges and beds of spring bulbs; later will come bedding plants to add new colors to the pattern, held together by the walls and other stonework. The landscape architects for this Glen Cove, Long Island, estate were the Olmstead Brothers.

141

Mild-climate gardening. Above, back again to Williamsburg, where superb specimens of boxwood have been collected. The boxwoods shown are venerable, but a fine effect can be obtained in remarkably few years by the gardener who starts with nursery-grown stock and a favorable climate.

At the right we are invited into a wall-enclosed garden in Charleston, South Carolina. The sweet alyssum spilling over the flagstone path permeates the air with fragrance and adds a further sense of intimacy.

142

144

Two contrasting gardens. The courtyard in a Palm Beach, Florida, garden at left is intimately tied to the house as much by planting as by location, becoming an outdoor living room that is practical as well as beautiful. Plants in pots—at this time, golden callas and marigolds set the color key—are an important part of the décor.

Above, a not too old formal garden in Scarsdale, New York—a garden in the English tradition. The flower borders of hardy bulbs and mixed perennials are arranged for bloom from early spring to fall. Once out through the gates of this walled garden, you are in a less formal setting: the landscaped area will give way to rolling meadows and naturalistic woodlands.

Landscape architect H. T. Lindeberg has created this entrance to a Middletown, Rhode Island, estate, which is dignified yet inviting. Perfect symmetry has been achieved by the correct use of plant material; there is no fear here of trees or shrubs growing beyond their allotted space.

Opposite, another illustration of the importance of understanding the habits of plant material, so essential in landscape art. The lush growth of elephant ears and other background plants has been taken into consideration. The raised side walls of the pool hold back encroaching growth, while the water surface is left comparatively open as a foil for the surrounding vegetation. This is a section of Mrs. Lorenzo E. Woodhouse's Palm Beach garden.

Three examples of the formal in landscape design, all intimately related to the architecture of the house. All three show the value of vines—in softening a formidable house front, in garlanding stonework.

These three photographs, like many others in this section, are the work of Samuel Gottscho, who has photographed most of the great gardens of America. Mr. Gottscho is also known for his photographs of wild flowers.

149

Hepaticas in a spring woodland. What man-invented dahlia or gigantic chrysanthemum can surpass the perfection of these wild flowers?

An expanse of lawn, a long perennial border that follows the stone wall —all viewed through the blossom-laden branches of an apple tree. No par-terres, no manicured borders, no clipped yews here, but what a stimulating yet relaxing landscape from one season to another. This is at Greenfield Hill, Fairfield, Connecticut.

Vistas—a disciplined hedge and grass-lined avenue open a path through flowering woodland, bringing incomparable naturalistic landscape within the boundaries of the garden.

152

A second vista—beyond the garden and into meadow and woods. Gardens are not all man-made. Nature herself is sometimes the best landscaper, creating both grand and modest effects. William Robinson, one of those who advocated no formal trifling with nature's handiwork, would have appreciated this scene as did Samuel Gottscho when he photographed it back in 1915.

153

Petunias, above, make a dooryard garden in California. Some kinds of petunias are sweetly scented, supplying yet another asset in addition to their ever-abundant crop of flowers.

There can't be too many daffodils as long as there are apple trees to plant them under. In their greatest crowds daffodils seem even more friendly, spreading their gold liberally. Their riches can become yours if you will plant a few bulbs each fall.

A naturalistic planting on the cottage, not estate, scale; the heart dances as happily with a dooryard full of daffodils as with a hillside full. Budding lilac and dogwood, too, say that spring has come to New England.

156

Making good use of the gnarled form of an ancient apple tree, the homely sturdiness of a stone fence. In this dappled shade you can find astilbe, primroses, day lilies and annual nicotiana. Other possibilities for planting in such a situation are the varied and interesting hostas (plantain lilies), ajuga, trailing myrtle (*Vinca minor*), Solomon's seal.

Fortunate is the gardener who can solve grading problems by creating a sunken garden. Gardens that are lower than the surrounding landscape can be just as interesting to the onlooker as gardens that rise. Variations in gardening, as in other pursuits, can be welcome if carried out with restraint and taste. The bulldozer is not always the solution.

Curves. A brooklet meandering along the foot of a sloping lawn, its outlines varied by well-placed stones, clumps of plants looking as if they happened to grow there. In the foreground the daisylike pyrethrum. Nature's ways with water can be duplicated—either grandly or modestly.

A flagstone path, curving like the brooklet, shows the essence of art in its casual paralleling of the pond's border. It is kept company by generous patches of bluebells, forget-me-nots, primroses, trollius. By the water's edge is a clump of moisture-loving iris.

This is the other end of the path on the preceding page, seen now through a canopy of arching lilacs. The repeated patches of spiked flowers are ajuga or bugle, an easy-to-establish dark blue perennial for shaded locations.

A curving wall, friendly rather than formidable, separates woodland from garden, yet serves as an easy transition between both areas. Daffodils inside the garden and outside the walls clearly belong in both worlds.

On the West Coast living and gardening are easy, informal. Shasta daisies peer over a picket fence, continue up a winding walk. Opposite, another daisy, the yellow Marguerite, makes a billowing hedge along a friendly porch. In such a setting gardening becomes mostly pleasure, maintenance is reduced to a minimum.

Whether springing from smooth turf or with their feet anchored in rocks, trees create the setting. They are plants beyond price, to be treasured, cared for, and cured when necessary (the apple arching over the tulip border bears honorable wounds, skillfully treated).

This rock garden is able to use both cultivated plants and wildings. In such a setting native ferns can be happy in a crevice next to plants that have been long in cultivation, perhaps improved by selective breeding or hybridizing. Actually the best rock gardens are born, not made. Nature, again, has proved herself to be the best architect, as a spring walk in any rocky woodland will show.

166

Contrast of forms and textures is everywhere important: conifers reaching toward the arching elms, with low-growing forms in the foreground; the varying heights and patterns of palms, the generous spread of ferns, the spidery growth of papyrus, and the flat calmness of pond lilies.

In the land of palms and the land of pines gardeners with an eye for nature can learn much of the art of landscaping—putting likes with likes, placing plants with tact as well as technical know-how—the result, a serenity, a rightness, that has much in common with natural settings.

169

There are specialists as busy seeking and helping to create new varieties of water lilies as the breeders who appear each season with new roses. The variety of water lily shown here is named Henry Snow.

Water lilies can make gardens of water, yuccas can make gardens of desert land. There is a plant for every climate, for every soil, for sun, and for shade.

170

Plants have a way with stones, a way of making themselves at home in the unlikeliest spots, softening and often scenting what otherwise would be an arid flight of steps, a dead level of pavement. Mother of thyme is the tradi-

tional fragrant herb for planting between flagstones; it and a few other spreading herbs don't mind being stepped on. A place where the ground slopes, creating two levels joined by steps, multiplies the landscape possibilities.

Steps can also be of stone. These stone steps are a happy link between the woodland and rocky ledges and the considerably more formal garden on the right, complete with columns and sundial.

174

The variations in steps are endless. They can be of wood, as are the peeled logs above, which are very much in harmony with the stone and timber house and its informal planting.

Paths that lead to the seaside or, supposedly, into the woods. Apart from having focus, these two gardens have little in common. The seaside garden in Miami, Florida, is full of rigid patterns; only the sea can be unpredictable.

The garden of pines and pieris is from *House Beautiful's* 1949 Pace Setter Garden at East Orange, New Jersey. Ethelbert Furlong was the landscape architect.

178

The pattern of woodwork—here in an unusual lath house—is effective both inside and out. Outdoors the precision of the design borders, indoors the sun and shadow patterns of palms and lattices are interestingly harmonious.

180

Midsummer in a garden in Mt. Kisco, New York. Everything is here—long vistas, wide expanses of smooth lawn, a gently gushing fountain in a circular pool surrounded by a mixture of perennials, now dominated by the ever-flowering day lily. And one or all of these features can be enjoyed from the rambling, comfortable porch.

Autumn comes to a garden in an old Connecticut apple orchard. The bed of primroses lying in the friendly shade of the far tree will be ready to flower again in the spring and will vie with the apple blossoms for attention.

VII

PROGRESS IN
PLANT SCIENCE

by P. P. Pirone

BECAUSE new medical discoveries and the development of more devastating implements of war have monopolized the front pages in recent years, few people realize that agriculture too has made great progress. In fact some farm and garden practices have changed more in the past fifteen years than in the previous fifteen hundred years—just as the plants have.

From agricultural research laboratories have already come chemicals that will speed up a plant's growth rate or slow it down; induce roots to form on stems or prevent the sprouting of tubers and bulbs in storage; help to set and hold fruits on trees or prevent the development of undesirable, unwanted ones on other trees; double the size of plants or keep them dwarfed; and make plants immune to attacks of insects and diseases. These are but a few of the things farmers and gardeners can already accomplish—things that almost rival Aladdin's magical lamp!

GROWTH REGULATORS MOST INTERESTING At the top of the list of "miracle" substances one might well place the group of chemicals known as growth modifiers or growth regulators. And although the first report on this type of substance is now twenty years old, the real spark was provided only twelve years ago by two friends of mine, Drs. Zimmerman and Hitchcock of

186

the Boyce Thompson Institute for Plant Research in Yonkers, New York. These eminent scientists were first to report on the growth-regulating properties of 2,4-Dichlorophenoxyacetic acid, popularly known as 2,4-D. Today 2,4-D is no longer a laboratory curiosity, but is being manufactured at the rate of twenty-eight million pounds a year.

Among the unusual properties of 2,4-D is its selectivity; that is, it has the ability to kill broad-leaved weeds growing among plants of the grass family without seriously harming the grasses. This unusual selective power is now being utilized by both the home gardener and the farmer. The gardener can control broad-leaved weeds like dandelions and plantain in his lawn without harming grasses like Kentucky blue or Merion blue. The farmer uses it to control broad-leaved weeds in his grain crops. As a matter of fact, in this country nearly twenty-five million acres of small grains and corn are now treated each year with 2,4-D. Controlling weeds by chemical power rather than by hand labor, therefore, is certainly welcomed by the farmer. Several important precautions must be observed when using weed killers containing 2,4-D. These precautions are listed on the container together with detailed directions for use.

Many other chemicals also have this highly selective ability to destroy some kinds of plants without harming others. Stoddard Solvent, long used as a dry-cleaning fluid, is now used to destroy weeds growing among young carrots and other plants of the parsley family including parsnips, dill, fennel, and celery.

MCP, or MCPA, is one of the most recently introduced selective weed killers for use on lawns. Like 2,4-D, it destroys broad-leaved weeds without harming the desirable grasses, and in addition does not harm established clover. One popular brand of this material is sold under the name D-Leet.

Selective weed killers that behave just the reverse of 2,4-D have also been developed. The material known as IPC or Chloro-IPC, for example, will control grasses and grassy weeds without hurting broad-leaved plants such as beets, cabbage, spinach, beans, kale, carrots, collards, and lettuce. And with the discovery of Alanap the vine crops have also joined the long list of food plants that can be safely weeded with the spray gun rather than with the hoe. The common varieties of cucumbers, muskmelons, and watermelons are tolerant of Alanap and hence can be weeded with it. For some mysterious reason, however, most kinds of squash are definitely injured by this chemical despite the fact that squash is a member of the same family.

PRE-EMERGENCE WEED KILLERS One of the most interesting weed killers also developed recently and already widely available in small packages for home garden use is Crag Herbicide I, a close relative of 2,4-D. This material is a pre-emergence weed killer; that is, it kills both germinating and very young weeds of such plants as chickweed, crab grass, pigweed, and purslane. It will not control weeds after they have gotten very large. Best of all it will not harm cultivated plants with well-established roots. It must be remembered that at the start of the treatment the soil must be free from any large, established weeds.

Another unusual property of Crag Herbicide I is that it is inactive when first appled to the soil but becomes effective as soon as soil microbes act on it to change it into 2,4-D.

Thus far Crag Herbicide I has found its greatest use in beds of established vegetables such as corn, lima and snap beans, asparagus, and small fruits such as strawberries and raspberries. It is also recommended as a pre-emergence weed killer around established shrubs and evergreens and in perennial flower beds, bulbs, and roses. A four-ounce package is sufficient to treat 3000 square feet of garden and one treatment will prevent regrowth of certain weeds for three to six weeks. Thus it is possible for a gardener to treat his vegetable garden and established flower borders, then go on vacation for three weeks without worrying about weeds overrunning his garden in the interim!

Several other materials capable of destroying germinating weed seeds have also been developed. Premerge and Sinox E, both so-called dinitro compounds, are effective in controlling weeds in gladiolus, particularly when these chemicals are sprayed on the soil just as the first gladiolus shoots emerge.

OTHER WEED KILLERS   Among some of the so-called general purpose weed killers available are:

Dalapon, a systemic weed killer used to destroy all kinds of vegetation along railroad rights of way. It is particularly effective against such grasses as Johnson, Bermuda, and quack, and shows exceptional promise in the control of the giant plume grass, *Phragmites communis.*

Goodrite NIX, which destroys small succulent weeds and has no growth modifying or soil-poisoning effect. It kills only the leaves it actually wets.

Karmex, designed to kill deep-rooted perennial weeds without causing any serious growth modifications to cultivated plants.

CONTROL OF WOODY WEEDS   Woody plants such as poison ivy, wild brambles, and undesirable trees and shrubs can be killed with 2,4,5-T or mixtures of 2,4-D and 2,4,5-T. Although these growth-modifying substances are extremely harmful to broad-leaved plants, they are not toxic to humans and animals when used at the recommended weed-killing rates.

The chemical 2,4,5-TP, sold under the name Silvex, is a close relative of 2,4-D and 2,4,5-T. It has several important attributes not shared by its close relatives. It does not cause severe distortions on such plants as cotton, and hence is less of a drift hazard. It also is more effective than related substances in destroying certain species of oaks.

Undesirable woody plants, particularly poison ivy, can also be destroyed with ammonium sulfamate (Ammate). This chemical is more practical to use on small city properties because there is no danger that its fumes will drift and damage nearby desirable plants, as is the case with 2,4-D and 2,4,5-T. Then, too, the usual amount of rinsing will remove all harmful residues from the spray tank and hose.

CRAB GRASS CONTROL IN LAWNS Crab grass is perhaps the most common lawn pest in many parts of the country. Although 2,4-D applied to young plants will give some control, several other chemicals do a better job.

The two more efficient types of crab-grass killers on the market contain either phenyl mercury compounds or cyanates. The former are more effective early in the season—June and early July—when the crab-grass plants are small. The latter work best when the plants are large and have begun to root at the nodes. Neither will cause any serious harm to the desirable grasses when used exactly as recommended by the manufacturers.

The gardener should bear in mind that the best preventive for crab grass is a good, vigorous stand of permanent grasses. Hence the chemicals should be used primarily to help in establishing a vigorous lawn. But the conditions that encourage crab grass must also be corrected.

Homeowners who plan to start a new lawn in the fall can be assured of a weed-free seedbed by using Garden Cyanamid three or four weeks prior to seeding the lawn. Five pounds of cyanamid evenly applied and lightly raked into the surface of each hundred square feet of seedbed will not only destroy crab grass and other seeds, but will also supply nitrogen and lime to the new lawn. Exact details for using cyanamid are printed on the packages.

WEEDS ARE EXPENSIVE A good portion of this chapter has been devoted to the use of unusual chemicals for weed control because weeds are important factors in our economy. They are second only to losses from erosion in total cost to our nation's farmers. Present annual weed losses total about five billion dollars. One authority claims that this annual burden could be cut in half if we could only persuade every farmer to make full use of the chemicals and apply the knowledge we already have.

ROOTING CUTTINGS WITH GROWTH-MODIFYING SUBSTANCES
Both farmer and home gardener have already put some other growth-modifying substances to good use.

Faster and better rootings of cuttings can be obtained by using synthetic hormone preparations containing indolebutyric acid (Hormodin, for example) and naphthalene-acetic acid and chemically related compounds (Rootone, for example). The amount of active ingredient varies in these preparations and the concentration to use depends on the plants being rooted. Those that root easily require a weaker concentration, those that are difficult to root a stronger one. Directions for use and lists of plants requiring specific concentrations are enclosed with each package of rooting powder.

OTHER UNUSUAL USES FOR PLANT HORMONES Many orchardists and even back-yard gardeners are sometimes plagued by the untimely dropping of nearly mature apples. This situation can be largely prevented by spraying the apple trees with a special hormone (Apple-Lok, App-L-Set, Fruitone, and Parmone, for example) several weeks before harvest. The active ingredients in some of these preparations, believe it or not, are the same as those used to root cuttings. Some of these same chemicals will also retard flower-petal fall of oriental cherries, thus enabling the gardener to enjoy them longer. Those containing naphthalene-acetic acid can also be used to reduce the shedding of leaves of cut Christmas greens such as holly. Holly branches dipped in this plant hormone will hold their berries and leaves ten days to two weeks longer than untreated branches.

Naphthalene-acetic acid and related compounds can also be used to produce fine-tasting, seedless tomatoes earlier in the season. A water spray of naphthalene acetamide will make the bright red berries develop on female holly trees even though the nearest male holly tree is miles away. In nature, of course, a male tree must be growing no farther away than a hundred feet or so in order to provide pollen via bees and other agents to fertilize the female flowers.

Additional uses for growth-modifying substances include thinning (reducing the number of flowers) on fruit trees and completely preventing fruit development. Spray thinning of apples (to get larger fruits) is now standard practice in many parts of the country with savings up to fifty dollars per acre in labor costs over hand thinning. Fruits on mulberries, horse chestnuts, and crab apples can be completely prevented from developing with some of these sprays.

Another interesting plant-modifying substance, alpha methoxyphenyl acetic acid (MOPA), is capable of moving from one plant to another via the roots. When placed on the leaves of one plant, MOPA is absorbed, moves down the stem into the roots, and then out of the roots into the soil. It is then readily absorbed by the roots of nearby plants and translocated to their leaves, where it checks growth. Only about nine hours are required for the

190

chemical to make the trip from one plant to another in sufficient amounts to produce this effect. It won't be long before scientists will put this interesting discovery to some important practical use!

MALEIC HYDRAZIDE   Maleic hydrazide, more popularly known as MH or MH 40, is perhaps the most remarkable of all chemicals yet developed for modern gardeners. In addition to its ability to control some important weeds like wild garlic, knotweed, and quack grass, and to prevent sprouting of potatoes and onions in storage, MH 40 has the unusual property of retarding growth without impairing the health of plants. The degree of retardation is directly proportional to the dosage.

The unusual growth-retarding property has already been put to practical use in treating grass around the edges of the lawn, in areas adjacent to flower beds, under trees, and along fences. It is not recommended for the entire lawn, because the several grass varieties in the average lawn react to it differently and a heavily used lawn will not respond favorably to it. Some grasses are retarded more than others, with the result that a treated lawn takes on a rather ragged appearance. In so far as home lawns are concerned, therefore, the use of MH 40 should be restricted to areas that are difficult to mow and to areas not subject to heavy traffic. A large amount of MH 40 is being used to retard grass growth along parkways, in cemeteries, golf-course roughs, airfields and other infrequently used grass areas, at a tremendous saving in maintenance costs.

Another important use for MH 40, not yet widely practiced, is in controlling the growth of certain hedge plants to reduce the number of clippings. From the homeowner's point of view established hedges like California privet have one highly undesirable characteristic—their fast rate of growth.

In some research tests at the New York Botanical Garden several years ago we found that a 0.5 per cent solution of MH 40 (Slo-Gro) applied to privet hedges would slow their growth sufficiently to require but one clipping for the entire summer. We applied the MH solution with a hand sprayer twice at three-week intervals. No permanent harm was noticeable in the treated plants more than a year after the treatment.

Many will agree that it is a lot easier to spray the hedge once or twice during the growing season than it is to wield hedge clippers every few weeks. The use of MH 40, however, will not make clippers obsolete. They still will be needed occasionally to shape up even MH-treated hedges.

A Canadian research worker reported satisfactory growth retardation, for several months, of the sharp-leaf willow (*Salix acutifolia*) and the common buckthorn hedge (*Rhamnus cathartica*) with a 0.1 per cent concentration of MH. He found that common privet required a 1.0 per cent concentration for satisfactory results. The latter was twice as strong as that found necessary by us to check the growth of California privet.

Some additional uses for MH are perhaps also worth mentioning. It can be used to prevent fruiting of ginkgo trees, the females of which produce evil-smelling fruits that make the tree most undesirable. With the fruit set prevented the female ginkgo becomes a fine tree, especially for sidewalk situations in the larger cities.

Submersion of unopened rosebuds for one minute in a MH solution retards the opening sufficiently to permit storage of cut roses for two to four weeks at normal refrigeration temperatures. Not only does this treatment increase the storage period, but more consumer satisfaction is assured because treated flowers last longer in the home.

Maleic hydrazide is said to be a safe chemical to use—almost as safe as common table salt! It should not be applied in combination with insecticides and fungicides.

Perhaps it is not too risky to forecast that maleic hydrazide and other growth inhibitors will soon find widespread use to delay flowering in early-blooming plants and thus enable them to escape damage from late spring frosts. Someday gardeners may even be able to change tender plants into frost-resistant ones merely by spraying them with certain plant hormones! Foundation plantings of trees and shrubs could be made more useful over a longer period of time if their growth could be slowed down by growth regulators of the MH type.

Most of the growth-regulating hormones isolated thus far either slow up or speed up cellular development, in addition, of course, to increasing frost resistance. Recently a team of University of Wisconsin horticulturists reported the isolation of a growth regulator that has the effect of maintaining normal cell development. This new growth regulator is capable of reducing abnormal cell growth caused by other regulators of the 2,4-D type. Not only was it found capable of reducing the injurious effects of 2,4-D, but it also reduced the abnormal cell growth caused by the crown-gall (plant-cancer) bacterium. Perhaps someday our scientists will find the hormone that will make human malignant tissues revert back to normal ones!

SOIL CONDITIONERS   In the two and a half years that synthetic soil conditioners have been on the market many a gardener has wondered why his neighbor's garden shows better results from their use than his own. Eying his own hard-packed clay and then the friable loam across the fence, he asks himself, or his neighbor, "Why?"

There are many reasons for the widely varying results secured with this newest addition to the gardener's shelf of wonder chemicals. The most common cause has been the use of materials incapable of doing the job claimed by a few unscrupulous manufacturers. But some failures were due to the human factor rather than the chemical. A lack of understanding as to what synthetic soil conditioners can and cannot do, as well as the failure to follow directions down to the minutest detail, were most frequently responsible.

Gardeners cannot expect miracles with them. As someone has aptly put it, "Conditioners can only condition soil in condition for conditioning."

The evidence accumulated thus far by reliable research workers and home gardeners is that most of the conditioners presently on the market will improve the structure of both heavy- and medium-textured soils.

HOW SOIL CONDITIONERS WORK   To try to explain the chemistry of synthetic soil conditioners to the home gardener would be difficult. In everyday language, though, we might say they have the capability of regrouping tiny clay particles into large clusters or aggregates. Because they are large, these aggregates increase the amount of air space in the soil. They transform tight, gummy clays into friable soils of crumblike structure. Such soils are more spongy and porous when wet. They allow air to penetrate more readily and water to percolate more quickly, thus providing conditions that favor better root development.

Synthetic conditioners have several important advantages over the natural conditioners derived from organic matter such as peat moss and manure. The clumps or aggregates formed by them are far more stable since they are not subject to decomposition by soil microorganisms. Organic matter has to be replenished frequently because the natural soil-conditioning agents in it are quickly broken down by the soil microflora. Additional advantages of the synthetic conditioners are that a little bit will go a long way and they do the "fixing" almost overnight.

But synthetic conditioners have their drawbacks too! They will not improve all soils. A sandy soil, for example, cannot be improved with them, whereas natural materials like peat moss, manures, and leaves will do so. Nor will they improve poor drainage caused by subsoil hardpans, rock ledges, and seepage.

The initial cost for a good synthetic conditioner may seem high. But the cost is not prohibitive when one considers the ease of handling and the many years of improved soil structure obtained by their use. The cost of using them is certainly justified on so-called problem soils where the value of the plant material is high or where the amount of conditioner necessary to do the job is low. They can be used even with the least expensive crops in a vegetable garden. It is possible, for example, to condition limited areas of heavy soils for plants like tomatoes, cabbages, and vine crops. Before setting out the plants

193

a circular area about 2 feet across and 6 inches deep can be treated with 2½ ounces of synthetic conditioner and a plant set in the center of the treated area a few days later. Excellent vegetables have been grown in heavy soils treated in this way.

Certain chemical soil conditioners in liquid form can be applied to the soil surface to prevent crusting and thus aid seedling emergence. Crusting after rains is especially prevalent in home gardens because such intensely cultivated soils lose their porous structure quickly.

Lastly it is well to remind gardeners that although synthetic conditioners, *rightly made and properly applied,* will do remarkable things to heavy clay soils, there is no substitute for good soil management.

PLANT FOODS   No one really knows when man first began to use plant foods, more commonly referred to as fertilizers, to grow better crops. Certainly there was no need for them in the distant past when most soils were still rich in natural elements. Their development has no doubt resulted from modern, intensive agricultural practices where so much is taken out by the growing plants and so little is returned to the soil by man.

The American Indian discovered that by placing a dead fish beneath a hill of corn he got better plants, and that plants grew better where brush had been burned. He knew this but didn't know the reasons why. We know now that the process of decomposition of the fish released nitrogen into the soil, the decaying of its bones yielded phosphorus, and the wood ashes left by brush fires contained potash. These are the three major nutrients required by plants and the ones now supplied in every bag of so-called complete chemical fertilizer. Since early in the present century complete plant foods in dry form containing varying proportions of these three major elements designated by numbers 5-10-5, 10-8-6, or 7-7-7, for example, have been used by the millions of tons by farmers and gardeners.

In the past few years, however, thousands of home gardeners and commercial growers of food and ornamental plants have switched to high analysis, quickly soluble, complete plant foods having a nitrogen-phosphorus-potash ratio of 23-21-17, 20-20-20, 19-22-16, or 15-30-15. Oddly enough, with but a few exceptions, the manufacturers of these concentrated plant foods offered them as supplements rather than substitutes for the old-fashioned dry fertilizers like 5-10-5.

One important advantage of the all-soluble, high-analysis fertilizers is that many of them can be sprayed directly on the foliage and thus supply some of the raw nutrients to the plant directly through the leaves. The material called Rapidgro was the first complete plant food on the market that could be safely used to supply nutrients through the leaves.

194

Several factors were responsible for the sudden popularity of high-analysis plant foods. They are quickly available to plants either through roots, bark, or leaves, depending on how they are applied. Plants respond more quickly, thus enabling the gardener to see improvements sooner. They are easy and pleasant to handle. Most of them are sold in dry form, a few as concentrated liquids, but they all must be either dissolved or diluted in water before use. They are practically odorless—those of us who have worked with animal manures really appreciate this characteristic. They are more efficient and hence there is less waste. The phosphorus in the concentrates, for example, is in a form more readily available to plants than the phosphorus found in superphosphate or in dry mixed plant foods containing superphosphate.

High analysis, completely soluble fertilizers can be distributed more evenly than dry fertilizers and can be applied at times when the size of the crops or the season prevents the application of dry fertilizers.

Of course the high-analysis plant foods are more expensive, unit for unit, than the older kinds, but that's because some of the ingredients, particularly the instantly soluble phosphates, are more expensive than the ingredients in dry fertilizers. Moreover practically every particle in them is usable—they contain no fillers or other inert materials. Packaging them in neat, easily handled containers also adds to their cost.

Concentrated fertilizers when properly dissolved or diluted in water can be used in many ways: as transplanting solutions around newly set plants; as starter solutions to be applied to seeds as sown; as a soak for seeds and bulbs prior to planting; as booster solutions to already established, partly grown plants; and finally as foliage sprays to growing plants. Details on specific uses are to be found on the packages. Not all concentrates are safe to use as foliage sprays. Most of those sold for use as foliage sprays can be combined with the newer organic insecticides and fungicides such as Malathion, DDT, and Ferbam, thus enabling the gardener to feed the plants and control plant pests in one operation. Here too manufacturers' directions should be followed carefully.

ADDITIONAL AIDS IN PLANT NUTRITION Another interesting introduction to the list of garden chemicals, sequestrene of iron, is proving more effective as a cure for chlorosis caused by unavailability of iron than the long-used iron sulfate or iron ammonium citrate. Sequestrene of iron is especially effective in curing chlorosis in ericaceous plants like andromeda, azalea, and rhododendron growing in acid soils. Chlorotic plants growing outdoors should be sprayed during the growing season with a solution containing four level tablespoonfuls of sequestrene of iron in three gallons of water. Results will not be immediately apparent, but complete greening of the leaves should occur within six weeks to two months and healthy growth should continue after the return to normal color.

Promising control of iron chlorosis in hydrangeas with sequestrene of iron has recently been reported in England. The green color of potted hydrangea plants was fully restored, in some cases within five days, by saturating the soil with a weak solution of the chemical. In other cases the color was restored after two or three weekly soil applications. The same treatment was effective with chlorotic *Primula obconica,* but after a longer interval.

Another new type of plant food soon to be obtainable by home gardeners is Uramite, a combination of urea and formaldehyde. This is a well-granulated material containing about 38 per cent nitrogen, three quarters of which is in slowly available form. Uramite is said to be an exceptionally "safe" nitrogen fertilizer, that is to say, single applications may be made at higher nitrogen levels than is possible with the more soluble forms of nitrogen. Hence a full year's nitrogen supply may be applied at one time. According to the manufacturer, Uramite is ideally suited for turf and other long-season crops, greenhouse plants, and crops grown in irrigated areas or regions of high rainfall.

The so-called minor or trace elements such as manganese, boron, zinc, copper, iron, and molybdenum are absolutely essential for healthy plant growth. Where any one or several of these are lacking or unavailable, plants will not make normal growth. Minor elements can be supplied to plants either as sprays on the foliage or on the soil (Es-Min-El, for example) and in specially made glass beads or frit known as F.T.E. (fritted trace elements). When such glass frit is mixed into the deficient soil it slowly makes available adequate amounts of the essential trace elements to the plants.

INSECTICIDES   DDT, the chemical insecticide in part responsible for the present revolution in gardening practices, was the most widely publicized chemical discovery of the twentieth century. Although available for more than sixty years, its remarkable properties as a bug killer were not discovered until 1940. Three years later American army officers dramatized that discovery by spraying DDT on the bodies and clothing of the people of Naples to destroy lice and thus prevent a murderous typhus epidemic from flaming in the newly liberated city.

Other more varied uses of DDT have been found since. But in the past few years its use in gardening has diminished greatly because some pests have become resistant to it, because it increases spider-mite populations on many plants, and because better materials have been found.

Malathion is perhaps the most important newcomer in the field of insect control to appear since the advent of DDT. It has been tested by thousands of back-yard gardeners and commercial growers and has been found to do everything claimed for it, and more. Besides controlling "hard to kill" insects such as adult Japanese beetles, scales, thrips, and white flies, it is also effective against many kinds of mites. It will even control leaf miners on birch, holly, and boxwood after the larvae burrow their way inside the leaves. Apparently enough of the chemical moves into the sprayed leaf to poison the larvae inside. In this respect it has the same property exhibited by another insecticide, Lindane. Thus the timing of the spray applications for leaf-miner control where either Malathion or Lindane is used is not as important as formerly.

Here are some other pests that are readily controlled by Malathion: aphids, mealy bugs four-lined plant bug, tarnished plant bug, rose leaf hopper, lace bugs, tent caterpillars, and a wide variety of scale insects. In all it is capable of controlling more than two hundred different kinds of insects on over fifty different commercial crops.

Although it is an organic phosphate, a class of chemicals normally considered very dangerous to handle, Malathion is described by the United States Department of Agriculture as "one of the safest insecticides to handle" in so far as toxicity to plants, pets, and humans is concerned.

A few plants like maidenhair and Boston ferns are injured by it. It does not appear to control the leaf nematode of chrysanthemums, at least at the regular dosages, anywhere near as well as its close but extremely dangerous relative, Parathion. The latter is not recommended for home garden use.

Malathion is available as a 4 per cent dust for applying dry, as a 25 per cent wettable powder, and a 50 per cent emulsion for spraying. It is also available in a few so-called all-purpose dusts, in which it is combined with other insecticides and fungicides.

Another close relative of Malathion, Chlorthion, will soon be available. This is said to have the same relatively low order of toxicity to humans and pets and the capability of controlling practically the same kinds of insects.

SPECIFIC CONTROLS FOR MITES   In recent years mites have become a major pest of many plants including arborvitae, birch, boxwood, cedar, cypress, hawthorn, hemlock, oak, peach, phlox, pine, rose, and spruce.

In addition to Malathion there are available several excellent chemicals developed specifically for mite control. These are sold under the trade names of Aramite, Dimite, and Ovotran.

Among other recently developed insecticides are Chlordane, Aldrin and Dieldrin, which are especially effective against insects that spend part of their life cycle in the soil, such as Japanese beetle grubs, ants, chinch bugs, May beetles, and rose chafers. Earlier formulations of these insecticides were in powdered form and therefore were difficult to apply at low dosages. They sometimes were also disagreeable to apply when in powdered form. They are now being mixed with a granulated carrier that makes them safer and easier to handle and can thus be applied with a lime or fertilizer spreader. In granulated form these insecticides will not stick to dry grass, but will settle to the soil surface, where they are more effective and are away from pets and children.

Soon it may also be possible to purchase mixtures of fertilizers and insecticides to feed plants and to control soil-infesting insects in a single operation. Fertilizer-Chlordane mixtures already have been used successfully to control white grubs, mole crickets, and wireworms in potatoes.

The most recent and interesting development in the field of insect control involves the use of so-called systemics. A systemic insecticide has the property of being absorbed by plants from a solution applied to the soil or to the leaves so that the plant sap is toxic to certain sucking and chewing insects.

The material sodium selenate, used for the past ten years by commercial growers, has the unusual ability of controlling the leaf nematode in chrysanthemums when supplied to the plants via the soil. Unfortunately it is quite deadly and soils treated with it cannot be used for many years to grow food crops.

One of the new systemic insecticides now available to commercial growers of ornamental plants has the tongue-twisting name octamethyl pyrophosphoramide, which is also sold under the more easily pronounced names Pestox and OMPA. Another of the new systemics is trialkyl triophosphate, known more commonly as Systox or demeton. A soil drench of Systox around outdoor chrysanthemums and roses is absorbed by the plants' roots and transported to the leaves, where it prevents the development of mites and aphids. Plants thus treated become continually toxic to the pests and there is no need for repeated applications as is the case with insecticidal sprays applied externally. No one can deny that this is indeed a novel way to control insects.

FUNGICIDES FOR DISEASE CONTROL   Progress in plant disease control has kept pace with developments in other related fields. Ever since the famine in Ireland in 1845, the direct result of a fungus disease that destroyed the entire potato crop in that country, man has become conscious of the importance of plant diseases in his environment. The accidental discovery in 1878 of what we now call Bordeaux mixture, as a control for many fungus diseases, lent further impetus to the development of sprays capable of confining and controlling plant-destroying fungi and bacteria.

Within the past dozen years a number of so-called organic fungicides have been found to be very effective in controlling certain fungus diseases. Ferbam (Fermate and Karbam Black) is widely used to control black spot of rose, apple scab, and other fungus diseases.

More recently the material Captan, originally developed under the number 406 at the New Jersey Agricultural Experiment Station, has become one of the leading organic fungicides for general disease control on a wide variety of crops. It has a low order of toxicity to warm-blooded animals and causes little to no skin irritation to sprayer operators. Like other organic fungicides such as Ferbam and Manzate, however, Captan is not effective in controlling powdery mildew diseases.

The most effective fungicide for mildew control is Mildex. Formerly sulphur compounds were about the only chemicals that could control this type of fungus. Powdery mildew on roses, chrysanthemums, phlox, beans, and vine crops can be eradicated by applying Mildex twice a week. In very rainy weather or under conditions favorable for mildew development additional applications may be necessary.

Other weapons for plant disease control include the antibiotics or the so-called wonder drugs. The first commercially available antibiotic for the control of specific plant diseases was cycloheximide, sold under the trade name Actidione. Turf diseases, mint rust and cherry leaf spot are three diseases which can be controlled with it.

The material Agrimycin, a combination of two well-known antibiotics, terramycin and streptomycin, appears, if the results of early tests are borne out, to provide us at long last with a practical way of combatting that highly destructive and widespread bacterial disease of apples, pears, hawthorns, and other rosaceous plants known as fire blight.

Of considerable interest to persons charged with the job of combatting plant diseases is the report of the isolation of a new antibiotic, oligomycin, which is said to control diseases caused by many kinds of fungi. Most of the antibiotics developed thus far, whether for humans or plants, are effective against diseases caused by bacteria. Some other antibiotics reported to be effective in the control of certain specific fungus diseases are thiolutin, fungicin, toximycin, helixin, and candicin.

As investigations proceed, more and more antibiotics will find their way into the field of plant disease control. Some of the names listed above may even get to be as common in the field of plant disease control as penicillin and streptomycin are in the field of human medicine today.

There are two important reasons why scientists are now going "all out" to investigate antibiotics for plant disease control. First, only a very tiny amount will give control—in some cases as little as a teaspoonful in one hundred gallons of water. Second, some antibiotics are systemic and hence can move throughout the plant's system. That means the entire plant will be protected as is the case with the several systemic insecticides mentioned earlier. Perhaps someday scientists may even discover a systemic fungicide-insecticide

199

combination that will control all the fungus diseases and insect pests of the plant that absorbs it!

No chapter that tells of the latest and most unusual discoveries in gardening would be complete without the admonition that not all the know-how of the world's greatest chemical laboratory is ever likely to devise a packaged substitute for good, old-fashioned common sense. Nor will any modern chemical aid to gardening ever substitute for the skill of the gardener.

VIII

THE KITCHEN GARDEN
MONTH BY MONTH

by F. F. Rockwell

WILL you be growing at least part of the vegetables you'll be eating this summer?

If you do, you'll find them of very much better table quality, you'll save some money, and you'll reap a harvest of fun and satisfaction as an extra dividend. If supreme table quality does mean something and if you would like to swap some spare time for dollars saved at the grocery store, then the game is worth considering.

First of all you do not need a big piece of ground. In fact you can grow vegetables that will pep up your summer menus considerably without having a separate vegetable plot at all. I know a woman who raises a large part of the summer vegetable supply for her family of three—and a goodly quantity of onions and the "makin's" of tomato juice and pickles for winter—by utilizing spots, at different periods, in a big, sunny perennial border on her town lot. Some of these vegetables are really decorative in themselves; others blend into the general flower-border scheme. Often it's possible to find a corner where a curved or an L-shaped vegetable plot may be fitted into the general garden design. A vegetable garden doesn't have to be rectangular, even though they are usually made that way.

202

What you do require for success in growing your own vegetables is the following:

1. SUNSHINE: Plenty for at least half of the daylight hours; even light shade is detrimental to most vegetables.

2. SOIL: rich and deep, or soil that can be made so. In the latter case somewhat more time and expense will be involved, but success can be achieved.

3. TIME: sufficient to attend to the work involved in planting, weeding, cultivating, and dusting or spraying crops that require protection. The time required will vary from an average of two hours a week for a very small garden to five or six for a fairly large one.

4. EQUIPMENT AND MATERIALS. The equipment required for a small garden need include practically nothing more than most suburban home-owners already possess, i.e., a digging fork (or spade), a hoe, rake, hand weeder, and a small hand dust gun. The materials will include seeds and plants, humus and fertilizers, and pesticides. For a small vegetable garden the additional cost, above that of growing flowers alone, need not exceed $3.00 to $5.00. It doesn't take many heads of lettuce and broccoli, or pounds of tomatoes and beans, at present prices, to repay that amount!

Let us turn back and look a bit further at the factors of sunshine, soil, and time. On many suburban places, where at first glance it may seem that no really sunny spot is to be found, a somewhat more careful search will reveal that such areas do exist, or may be made, by the simple expedient of doing some pruning, or, in exceptional cases, removing a tree. I have the greatest admiration and love for fine trees, but I have known hundreds of instances where a big tree has been kept for years at too great a sacrifice in terms of the injury it did, through dense shade and food- and moisture-robbing roots, to the garden as a whole. This is not to suggest that anyone should cut down a fine and well-located tree in order to grow a few vegetables—far from it. But not all big trees are assets.

We spoke of a "rich, deep soil." A rich soil is one capable of producing a vigorous growth of plants. In these days there are few home sites, new or old, that, unaided, will produce such growth. On the whole it takes better soil to grow really good crops of vegetables than is required to get satisfactory results with flowers. This means, especially for root crops such as beets, carrots, and parsnips, a soil that is mellow and enriched for at least 8 inches deep, and preferably 2 to 4 inches deeper. It takes two or three years to build such a soil where that is necessary, but all except the poorest of soils may be coaxed into yielding satisfactory crops of most vegetables even the first season or two by the addition of humus and fertilizers. Stable manure is the best source of humus, but it is becoming more and more difficult to obtain. Satisfactory—and much more easily handled—substitutes may be had in the form of peat moss, and in the dehydrated manures sold under various trade names. Homemade compost is another invaluable source of humus, as are also green-manure crops, which are dug under where they grow.

WHAT SIZE GARDEN? If you decide to grow your own vegetables this summer, your first problem will be to decide how much of a garden you should undertake. In most cases the two limiting factors are space and time.

If you have abundant room but limited time, it may be advisable to space the vegetable rows much farther apart than usual. This will permit the use of power tools. These are being constantly improved in design, to make them more practical for use in comparatively small areas.

The season when planting can be begun may seem weeks away, but it is none too early to start in midwinter on the making of a definite plan of just what you expect to undertake. Measure accurately the size and the shape of the area you expect to use. Get a few sheets of cross-ruled paper (you'll need more than one if it's your first attempt!), draw the area to scale, and arrange your plantings. The spaces between rows should be all minimal; they can be made wider, but not narrower. Closely spaced rows have the advantage of shading the soil, thus conserving moisture and checking weed growth; but they require cultivation by hand.

One great advantage of a carefully worked-out plan is that it will save much time in planting; another is that it saves waste in seed and plant buying.

If you are "growing your own," select your vegetables primarily on the basis of table quality. Of course there are other factors to be considered such as good yield, earliness, and resistance to insects and diseases. But most home gardeners grow vegetables in order to get better ones than they can buy. Usually they can save some money, also, thus making the venture doubly attractive.

The commercial grower's reasons for selecting his varieties are quite different, he being chiefly concerned with eye appeal, shipping quality, and big yields. It is to his advantage to have a crop mature all at one time, or as nearly so as possible. For the home gardener, however, a short crop season of an all-ready-at-once variety is a drawback rather than an advantage.

Earliness, too, is very important to the commercial grower. The market price of a crop such as tomatoes or sweet corn may fall as much as 50 per cent in a few days. As a rule, extra-early varieties are of inferior table quality. Moreover the earliest varieties of vegetables that ordinarily yield or remain in good condition over a fairly long period—such as tomatoes, peas, cucumbers, squash, lettuce, and cabbage—"go by" much more quickly than the main crop sorts. In planting these the home gardener sacrifices more than he gains.

A word as to "novelties"—varieties of current or very recent introduction! The seed business being what it is, the catalogue makers each year feature wondrous introductions, in almost every case claimed to be better than any existing variety. A few of these wonder vegetables stick and in the course of time become standard varieties; most of them soon drop out. By all means try some of the novelties, especially those that have won an award by the All-America Selections Committee—an organization that annually conducts nationwide tests of new vegetables and flowers before they are introduced. But do not give up a satisfactory old variety until you have grown the supposedly superior one alongside it.

The home vegetable varieties recommended in the following list are not claimed as necessarily the best, but are the ones that, as a result of many years of trial and error in our own garden and observation in other sections, my wife and I grow. They make a good, sound list for the beginner to consider as he checks through his catalogues.

Asparagus. Mary Washington, rust resistant, tops the list. The different strains vary but slightly.

Bush Beans. Of the several comparatively new bush beans we still like *Tendergreen* best. Topcrop, a few days earlier, is also excellent. If you like yellow-podded beans, try Surecrop wax (Golden Bountiful). *Lima Beans* are of two distinct types: large-seeded and small-seeded or "baby." Of the former Fordhook 242 is the standard. Of the latter a new U.S.D.A. variety, Peerless, seems to justify the name.

Pole beans include both "snaps" and limas. Of the former Kentucky Wonder (Old Homestead) has remained unchallenged for more than half a century. The new Burpee Golden, with wide, flat pods instead of round ones, we grew for the first time last year, and consider it the most delicious of all pole beans. Pole limas, like bush limas, are large- and small-seeded. Of the former we like best Big-6 and Ideal; Sieva or Butter Bean, largely grown in the South, is the standard small-seeded variety.

Beets. Except for trials of new varieties we grow only Lutz Green-Leaf (Long Season; Winter Keeper), which is delicious at any stage from thumbnail size to full grown. Two sowings, one in early spring and another in June, will provide sweet, tender-fleshed beets all summer, fall, and through the winter. The young foliage makes especially delicious beet greens.

Broccoli, more easily grown than cabbage, an excellent crop for freezing, and yielding several cuttings, is one of the indispensables. Green Mountain, early Waltham 29 are more uniform than Calabrese.

Brussels sprouts. Catskill is more compact and earlier than the standard Long Island Improved.

Cabbage. For earliness and table quality we still like old Early Jersey Wakefield, but with many gardeners Golden Acre is a favorite. For the home gardener the new Bonanza is really that, for it forms compact, small heads that will stand without splitting for weeks. (In sections where the yellows disease is prevalent, plant only disease-resistant kinds.)

Cabbage, Chinese (or *Chinese celery*) makes long, loose cabbagelike heads, but it is not true cabbage. Michihli is the preferred variety.

Cauliflower. Early Purple Head is much more easily grown than the white sorts, and is of excellent flavor. Snowball and Early Snowball, of which there are as many improved strains as there are seedsmen, are the standard varieties.

Carrots. The kind to grow depends largely on your soil. A short-rooted variety, such as Nantes Half-long, is best for shallow or stony soils.

Celery. Our favorite variety here at Grayrock is still the nutty, thick-stalked Emperor (Fordhook). Utah and Cornell 19 (or the new Cornell 619) are better known.

Corn. Sweet corns, like field corns, vary greatly in their adaptability to different sections; hence there is wide divergence in their standing in various parts of the country. Golden Cross Bantam (eighty-five to ninety days) is the most universally liked. North Star is an excellent extra-early—about seventy days. Marcross is a few days later. For a main crop I like Lincoln—about a week later. Golden Midget is well worth growing in the very small garden.

Cucumbers. Disease resistance, resulting in a long-season yield, is important for the home gardener. Burpee Hybrid and the similar Sensation Hybrid lead in this respect. China is an ideal variety for growing against a trellis or fence.

Eggplant. For short-season climates the hybrid varieties, Black Magic and Burpee, are better than the standard Black Beauty.

Endive. Deep Heart (Full Heart) is the best of the curly-leaved types. Witloof (French endive) is forced for winter salad.

Leek. Excellent, winter-hardy, and much easier to grow than the related onion. Leek should be tried by more home gardeners. We have never found much difference among the varieties offered, but the new Swiss Special, which we have not yet grown, is claimed to be the largest.

Lettuce. We've tried most of the new ones, but Mignonette would still be our choice if we grew only one variety. Oakleaf would be next. Salad Bowl is good through most of the summer. Penlake is a reliable cabbage-head sort, if you prefer that type. Bibb is of extra-fine quality, but in many sections not too dependable. Great Lakes is one that is always good.

Melons. Among cantaloupes (muskmelons) we find Delicious the best bet. Honey (Sugar) Rock is smaller and slightly earlier. Among watermelons choice depends largely upon climate. New Hampshire Midget is the earliest, with Honey Cream (Golden Sweet), yellow fleshed, a close second. Klondike is a good-flavored later sort.

Onion is often difficult from seed; get sets or plants by named variety if possible. Crystal (Bermuda) White Wax, Early and Sweet Spanish, are mild-flavored and good for scallions. The Globe varieties, yellow, red, and white, are much better winter keepers. The Evergreen (Japanese) bunching onions are rather tough. For growing from seed try one of the new hybrid strains.

Parsnip. The several varieties are much alike. Paramount is perhaps the best.

Peas. There are many varieties, with slight differences. Our choices are Mammoth Pod Extra Early and Alderman (Dark-Seeded Telephone) for main crop. For a later crop or in hot climates use Wando.

Pepper. For an early, mild pepper, plant Sunnybrook or Penn Wonder; for a "bull nose" type (for stuffing) California Wonder; really hot (for flavoring) Hungarian Wax or Long Red Cayenne.

Potato. Consult local gardeners for varieties that do well in your locality. Our favorites are Chippewa, early; and Kennebeck for main crop.

Spinach. America is best crinkle-leaved variety; Viking, best smooth-leaved. For summer use New Zealand, not a true spinach, is good, and bears continuous cropping.

Squash. If only one is grown, use Butternut, good during summer, yet an excellent keeper. For summer only plant Crystal Bell, a pattypan type, and Caserta or black (Fordhook) zucchini.

Tomato. Don't waste space on extra-early varieties; Burpee Hybrid or a similar hybrid for early use and reliable Rutgers or Marglobe for later will keep the table supplied. For a big tomato we like Big Boy, which is smoother than other two-pounders.

Turnip. Golden Ball is the standard variety for summer use. Of the Swede turnips (rutabagas) for fall and winter, Alta Sweet, a Canadian variety, is tops in quality.

When as a teen-age youngster I first began growing vegetables, I could not understand how the local market gardeners always managed to have their crops mature so much earlier than mine. That, of course, was in the days before truckloads and trainloads of perishables—such as lettuce, radishes, green onions, beets, and peas—from California and Florida supplied local markets even through the winter months.

A little investigation soon revealed the two main reasons. First, these local vegetable growers began sowing long before I had considered it safe to risk putting seeds in the ground. Second, for the earliest crops they set out growing plants of many kinds that I grew only from seed.

When I began to put this newly acquired information to use, to my surprise I discovered that many vegetables actually prefer the cold wet weather of early spring, and make much better growth than later on. I had learned the first step to successful vegetable growing.

The following are plants that prefer or will tolerate cool weather: beets, broccoli, cabbage, carrots, cauliflower, endive (Witloof), kohlrabi, leek, lettuce plant, lettuce seed, onion seed, onion seedlings, parsley, parsnips, peas (smooth or wrinkled), potatoes, radishes, Swiss chard, turnips. Any of these may be planted in the open as soon as the soil is in condition to be prepared; that is, as soon as it will readily crumble when dug or plowed. (A simple test to determine this is to squeeze a handful of dug soil into a ball: if, under slight pressure, it crumbles apart readily, it is fit to work; if it tends to remain a wet, soggy mass, wait a bit longer before beginning operations.) Both drainage and the amount of humus the soil contains will have much to do with its "earliness"; for instance, clay soils are late soils unless the humus content is very high.

For earliest harvest a number of these hardy vegetables may be set out as growing plants. They may be purchased from local garden shops or seeds-men; or the gardener, as he gains experience, may wish to grow his own. For a small garden it is not a difficult matter to start a few dozen seedlings indoors, and later transfer them to a cold frame that will provide protection from late hard frosts.

In order to grow good seedlings, however, it is absolutely essential to have an abundance of direct sunshine, or, as a substitute for it, controlled electric lighting. While seeds are germinating in a temperature of 60° to 70°, no light is needed. Immediately after they have germinated, full light is essential. A day or two's neglect once they are above ground may render them next to worthless.

One great advantage of growing your own plants is that you can get exactly the varieties you want. Another is that the plants will be on hand, ready to set out when conditions are most favorable. Even the beginner will do well to try growing at least a few plants, thus acquiring a new skill that will be very useful in all his gardening work.

When buying plants, do not be influenced by size alone. Short, stocky plants, with dark, tough-looking foliage, that have been hardened by a period of exposure to outdoor weather are much to be preferred to those with soft, lush foliage taken direct from a greenhouse.

Success with vegetables depends to a great extent on what is done before they are planted. If the soil is not properly prepared in advance, no amount of aftercare and fertilizing will make up for this neglect. No "miracle" soil treatment or foliar feeding alone is going to produce maximum crops.

Proper soil preparation includes consideration of three distinct factors: mechanical condition, humus content, and plant food. I have often referred to this combination as the gardener's milking stool—a very firm foundation if it has all three legs, but more or less useless if any one leg is missing.

The first of these foundations is mechanical condition. Soil for vegetables should be dug or plowed at least 8 inches deep, better 10 or 12 inches, and so pulverized as to be of uniform texture with no hard lumps, and free from stones and roots. This is especially important where root crops are to be grown. Once clayey soil has been well worked, chemical soil conditioner will help to keep it in good condition longer.

The second leg, humus content, is provided by organic matter. In former days this was usually supplied by stable manures, but since automobiles do not provide this commodity, we must now depend upon compost, "green" manures (crops grown to be dug under to decay in the soil), and humus purchased in the form of peat moss, prepared peat soils, or commercial (dried) manures. This matter of humus is usually the weak leg, the one the beginning gardener neglects. Get all the humus-making materials, of any kind, that you possibly can. Humus keeps the soil porous and open, ready to absorb and to hold moisture, warmer in cold weather and cooler in hot, and easy to cultivate.

Plant food, the third essential, is more easily provided. For garden purposes any high-grade complete fertilizer will do. Standard analyses vary according to soil conditions in different sections: 5-10-5 and 4-8-12 (the figures indicating ratios of nitrogen, phosphoric acid, and potash), are those commonly encountered.

To prepare a vegetable plot, first, dig deep and pulverize the soil well; next, spread on humus-making material (2 inches or more of compost, peat moss, or its equivalent) and cultivate in as deep as you can; and last, add 3 to 5 pounds of fertilizer per 100 square feet whether you are planting vegetable seeds or plants or both.

After the soil has been dug and enriched, the surface should be leveled and smoothed by a final going over with an iron rake. On new soil this will usually require two operations; the first to remove any remaining roots and stones, the second to get a really fine, smooth surface. As small seeds are covered only ¼ to ½ inch, and as good germination depends largely upon having the soil in close contact with the seeds, this is most important.

It will both save time and assure a neater job if labels are prepared in advance and put in place exactly where each row is to go, according to a prepared planting plan. Now stretch a stout garden line as a guide, and mark the rows with a pointed stick along it. For very small seeds the corner of a hoe (often advocated for this job) is much too large. Keep all rows perfectly straight and parallel. This is not merely a matter of neatness; it will be of great advantage in subsequent weeding and cultivating.

Do not sow seeds too thickly. To do so only means extra work in thinning out after the plants are up. With the back of a narrow-bladed hoe firm seeds into the soil before covering to assure close contact. Then pull fine soil over the seeds to required depth, tamping down only lightly.

Larger seeds, such as peas and corn, are planted in furrows 2 to 4 inches deep. For early plantings cover only 1 to 2 inches deep at first, and then fill in as the plants grow.

If you decide to set out plants—cabbage, broccoli, cauliflower, lettuce —make sure that they have been well hardened. Mark off positions in row; dig out a good trowel-size hole at each point and in the bottom mix thoroughly a trowel full of a mixture of three parts dried manure and one part bone meal; refill hole with loose soil and set plant. Press the soil around its roots very firmly, and deep enough so first leaves are just above ground level. If soil is at all dry, water thoroughly in hole before planting.

In case unexpected hard freezing weather threatens, plants may be protected by covering temporarily with plastic domes, Hotkaps, or even newspaper tents held in place by soil.

With early planting finished the gardener can relax, so far as his vegetable plot is concerned, for a few weeks. Chances are, though, that he will not! Instead he'll be poking in the soil to see if his seeds are beginning to sprout.

May, for most parts of the country, is the vegetable grower's busiest month. The seeds of the early hardy crops that were sown a month or so ago will have germinated and made sufficient growth to be thinned out—an operation that cannot be postponed without disastrous results. And as the ground warms up and danger of late frost recedes, planting of the tender vegetables— those that will not withstand even a slight freeze—can be started.

Then, too, there are a few insect pests that may be encountered even early in the season, and these must be watched for and given battle as soon as they appear. And such time as the gardener may have after attending to these duties will be required for cultivating and otherwise tending his growing plants. Yes, May is indeed a busy time for the vegetable grower, but an enjoyable one, too, for it is the pleasantest season of the year for garden work, and some of the products of his earlier efforts will be ready for harvesting.

THINNING   The one garden operation that the beginner is most likely to neglect, or to do inadequately, is that of thinning out such crops as are sown and grown in rows. Because seed germination is at best an uncertain matter, it is necessary to sow seeds of such vegetables as lettuce, spinach, beets, carrots, onions, and the like much more thickly than the plants can be grown. With lettuce, for instance, several seeds are sown to the inch, whereas the plants, to develop properly, require from six to twelve inches to develop full-size heads.

The sooner thinning can be begun after the plants are safely up and established—that is, when the second or third true set of leaves has begun to develop—the better. If thinning is delayed beyond this point, the job becomes much more difficult and time-consuming, and the roots of the plants that are to be left must be disturbed to a greater degree.

In the home vegetable patch the operation of thinning is usually done in two bites. Plants are thinned out first to about half the required distance. By the time the second thinning is required, such vegetables as may be used in an immature state—any of those mentioned above, for instance—will be large enough to be taken to the kitchen. Unless you have eaten baby beets (cooked with the tender tops on), fingerling carrots, and half-grown spinach, you do not know quite how delectable these vegetables can be. Some others —parsnips and salsify, for instance—do not yield this extra bonus, so these are thinned out to the full distance at one time. Peas, on the other hand, seldom require thinning.

As the thinning is done, any weeds that may have started in the row are removed. Take care to get them out by the roots; otherwise they will sprout again and be four times as difficult to remove.

After thinning and weeding cultivate the soil between the rows, using a light hand hoe, a scuffle hoe, or a hand cultivator. This will loosen the packed soil and leave the surface loose and in condition to absorb and hold rain.

While the soil is still cold, early in the season, nitrogen, even if present in sufficient supply, may not be available to the hungry plant roots. It is advisable therefore to sprinkle nitrate of soda or aluminum sulphate along the rows, using about two pounds per hundred square feet. Apply just before a rain if possible; otherwise be very careful not to get any on the foliage. This extra nitrogen is an excellent booster for leaf vegetables such as spinach and lettuce; and also helpful in giving root crops a vigorous start.

If peas are being grown, get brush or other support for them in place before they begin to fall over.

TENDER CROPS   The tender vegetables are of two types: those grown from seed and those of which plants are set out. The former include corn, beans, and the various vine crops; the latter, tomato, eggplant, and peppers.

Corn can be planted when temperatures no longer fall below freezing; bush beans about a week later. Lima beans and the vine crops—squash, cucumbers, and melons—are heat lovers and nothing is gained by planting them before the soil has really warmed up. The use of paper or plastic tents (sold as Hotkaps, Plant Domes, etc.), enables the gardener to plant a week or two earlier. This not only gives them a running start, in northern sections, but also protection from insect pests during their early growth.

An extra row or two of early corn or beans may be had by planting in a furrow 3 to 4 inches deep, and covering the seed only 1 to 2 inches. If a frost threatens after seeds have sprouted, loose soil hoed in over them will afford temporary protection.

Succession plantings of such early vegetables as lettuce, radishes, and peas may be made in regions where temperatures remain fairly cool; New Zealand spinach, a hot-weather plant, may pinch-hit for spinach where mid-summer weather is very hot; and second plantings of beets and carrots should go in toward the end of May or June.

SETTING OUT TENDER PLANTS   Getting a good start with the tender vegetables that are set out as growing plants—tomato, eggplant, and pepper —depends on the treatment they receive for the week or two after they are out. At this season of the year sudden spells of heat and high winds are likely to be encountered. Therefore, try to do your planting just before—or during— a showery day.

If planting must be done during unfavorable weather, do the job late in the afternoon. Water the bottoms of planting holes very thoroughly before setting out plants, and protect tops from hot sun with newspaper tents, open at both ends to permit free circulation of air. Plants that wilt badly after planting will eventually recover, but the severe check may delay first pickings.

In order to economize on space and to get better fruits, tomatoes in the home garden are usually provided some sort of support. Whether this be a trellis, wires, or individual stakes, have the supports in place before setting out the plants. The job can be done in much less time, and without danger of injuring the plants. It is wise to provide strong supports, as the weight of the vines is considerable.

EARLY PESTS   While the majority of plant pests and diseases are not likely to appear before warm weather, there are a few early-season ones that the vegetable gardener should be on the watch for. Among these are:

Aphids or plant lice, of several species—soft-bodied sucking insects that usually appear first at the growing tips of stems and on undersides of leaves. The spring varieties are usually green or black. Watch peas, cabbage, and broad beans for any curling or twisted leaves. To control, spray with nicotine sulphate or spray or dust with pyrethrum or rotenone.

212

If you find a newly set cabbage or tomato plant or a juicy seedling neatly cut off at or just above ground level, the culprit is likely to be a dull, dirt-colored, soft-bodied fat worm, up to 2 inches long, who carries on this nefarious saboteuring activity during the night. An early morning search in the surface soil around the stem will usually reveal him. There are likely to be others, however, so it is well to apply at once poison cut-worm bait. This can be bought, or concocted at home by mixing one tablespoon each of arsenate of lead and of molasses with one cupful of bran. Tar-paper collars or used plant bands set at least one inch deep in the soil around newly set-out plants are also effective.

Flea beetles are small, dark insects that appear early in the season and hop gaily about on tomato, eggplant, cabbage, and other vegetables, puncturing tiny holes in the leaves. To control, dust with rotenone.

Root maggots are most troublesome to the cabbage group and to onions. Plants that wilt suddenly and come up at the slightest pull indicate their presence. They are small, dirty white maggots that destroy the feeding roots, or eat their way into fleshy underground stems or bulbs. Cabbage, broccoli, and cauliflower plants may be protected by fitting 3-inch disks or squares of tarpaper around the stems at ground level at the time of planting. Another control is to make a slight depression about the plant or along the row, and drench the soil with nicotine sulphate solution (one teaspoonful to one gallon of water) using one cupful to two plants or to three feet of row.

In June the vegetable garden really begins to pay dividends. Radishes, spinach, lettuce, green onions, peas, turnips, beet greens, and others will be in good supply, and—if you got an early start—even broccoli and cabbage before the end of the month. So the gardener is inclined to take it easy and rest on his oars. But if he wants to continue having a plentiful harvest right up to hard freezing weather, he must plan ahead and do more planting soon.

Succession plantings, as the term implies, are those that are put in to replace crops of the same kind that have been, or will be, used up before the summer is over. In the case of vegetables that must have cool weather—such as peas, spinach, and lettuce—it is not advisable to make late plantings unless one happens to live in a cool climate or at a fairly high altitude. For many of these, however, there are substitutes available. Beets and carrots may be planted at any time. A second sowing, put in before the end of the month, will provide a late-season supply. We like Lutz Green-Leaf (Long Season) beets and a long-rooted carrot such as Tendersweet. (On shallow soil, Nantes Half-long would be a better bet.)

Beans, which grow quickly, should be planted now and, if your growing season is a fairly long one, again in mid-July. Lima beans require longer to mature, but a dwarf-bush variety like Fordhook 242 will make it by frost.

Corn, which yields for but a short season, must be planted every two or three weeks to maintain a constant supply. Early varieties can be put in up to the Fourth of July; in southern gardens even a week or two later.

Lettuce likes cool weather, but there are some heat-resistant varieties. For a late sowing try the new Salad Bowl or Slobolt. Peas also like really cool weather. Our first planting came up this spring on March 10! A new variety, Wando, will stand much higher temperatures than any of the older sorts.

Spinach just will not thrive in hot weather, but in New Zealand spinach (really not a spinach at all) we have an excellent substitute; and it may be cut continuously up until frost.

Cucumbers often play out or are vanquished by disease before the end of the season. If you like them, make a second planting now—at a distance from the first planting if possible—to provide a late crop and little ones for pickling.

Cabbage and its close relatives, broccoli and cauliflower, will be gone before the end of the season. Sow seed of these and the winter cousins, Brussels sprouts and kale, now to provide plants for setting out about mid-July. Sprouts and kale, which thrive on frost, will yield until Christmas or later.

KEEP THEM GROWING   Important routine jobs for the month, upon which success with the crops already planted will depend, are cultivating, watering, and mulching. The more of the last of these you can do, the less time you will have to give to either of the former.

The object of cultivating is to keep the surface soil loose and friable, so that both rain and water can penetrate it readily, and the growth of weeds will be discouraged. Mulching accomplishes both of these purposes. You can use coarse compost, peat moss, buckwheat hulls, sawdust, or straw. A 2-inch layer is sufficient for most purposes.

Watering is necessary only when the soil becomes dry to a depth of several inches. If you must water, soak the soil thoroughly; a light sprinkling is wasted effort and may even be harmful instead of beneficial. A mulch conserves soil moisture to a remarkable degree.

The insect pests most likely to prove bothersome at this time are bean beetles; cucumber beetles (which also attack melons); squash bugs; cornstalk borer, and corn-ear worm; and squash borer.

Keep a constant watch for these invaders. Nowhere does the old adage that a stitch in time saves nine hold more true than in the control of pests and diseases. For bean beetles and squash bugs, use rotenone or methoxychlor; for cucumber beetles, rotenone; for cornstalk borer and ear worm, DDT dust. The modern all-purpose garden dusts and sprays control most pests you are likely to encounter, if you use them according to directions and in time.

IX

TREES

by Robert S. Lemmon

Drawings by Allianora Rosse

COLORADO SPRUCE
(*Picea pungens*)

Rigidly straight and formal, statuesque, densely needled, the Colorado spruce is one of America's most notable conifers. In its native home among the Rockies from Wyoming, Utah, and Colorado southward to New Mexico it may tower 100 feet above the ground, for it is a high-country tree and would have little use for the easier life of southern lowlands. In such rugged surroundings its color, which varies from a somewhat bluish green to a pale, silvery gray blue, finds a perfect setting.

Many years ago this remarkable evergreen attracted the attention of nurserymen because of its outstanding appearance, and its reception by the public in the Northeast quickly became cordial and widespread. Today it is the most popular of the spruces. Much of this enthusiasm is deserved, but it has blinded many homeowners to certain basic facts. As a result we now see countless Colorado spruces, usually under the pseudonym blue spruce, that are more of a blot on the nearby landscape than they are an asset. Let me explain: In the first place, we are dealing with a really big tree that is as out of place in an average lawn or front yard as a whale in a goldfish bowl. This would be bad enough if the Colorado's color were an ordinary green, but the marked infusion of blue, which characterizes its needles, simply serves to call extra attention to it.

Colorado spruces are really geared to the wide-open spaces, and under these conditions they can be used with superb effect. Several specific placements immediately come to mind. First, a group of four or five, well spaced to allow for future growth, in a far corner of a large open field to create a bold skyline accent. Second, an occasional specimen in front of a distant woodland to relieve its sameness with a point of color contrast. And again, on really spacious landscaped grounds, a differently colored distant strong point to key up other features.

You will notice at once that the needles are stiff, rather long, and very closely spaced. Each needle retains its life and color for seven or eight years, so you can see why the tree as a whole presents such a dense appearance.

The tan-colored cones are handsome, too, as they hang from the branchlets in true spruce fashion. Some of the larger ones may be 4 inches long, and since they cling to their places throughout the winter you can depend upon their heartening picture on any dreary day. Of course they do not appear until the tree is of some size—perhaps a dozen feet or so tall. But from then on the spruce's cones are an annual occurrence.

TULIP POPLAR
(*Liriodendron tulipifera*)

Whether you know it as tulip poplar, whitewood, tulip tree, yellow poplar, or simply poplar, it is the same handsome giant, straight as a flagpole, with yellow-green and orange tuliplike blossoms nestling in June among big, four-lobed leaves that turn to glowing yellow when autumn comes.

It has been rightly said that a tulip poplar needs a circle of ground space 75 feet across in order to develop its potential height of 100 feet or more and branch spread of 60-odd. Obviously it is not a tree for small properties, despite the fact that for its size it is remarkably trim and free from littering habits. Usually, too, its lowest branches are far enough from the ground to permit a good lawn turf beneath them.

It requires little save a moderately rich, dampish soil and an average climate with a winter minimum temperature never lower than 10–15 degrees below zero.

The trait of speedy growth is of importance if you are thinking of bringing in a seedling tulip tree from the fields or woods—an opportunity that frequently arises within the tree's natural range, for it is a generous self-sower. The success of the operation can be almost guaranteed in early spring if you select one not over a couple of feet tall and are careful to take up its deep-striking taproot intact.

It is the nature of the tulip poplar to be symmetrical despite its size and the heavy burden of leaves it carries, for its wood, though somewhat soft, is tough and the limbs are well designed and firmly anchored.

While a tulip tree is at its best during the foliage season, there is no time of year when it is without distinctive interest because of its flowers, branch pattern, and the whole tree's color changes.

218

219

JAPANESE MAPLE
(Acer palmatum)

This low, shrubby tree has been known and grown in the United States for well over a hundred years and is still going strong. It is the most satisfactory plant for certain important landscaping roles provided you secure one of its better forms. As a species, it is subject to great variation in leaf color and shape as well as character of growth, and you cannot be sure of how one will turn out eventually if it has been grown from seed. Here is perhaps the chief reason why a beautifully red small one so often disappoints its owner by turning green after a few years.

The scientific name of the Japanese maple, *Acer palmatum,* refers to the extremely divided or "palmate" outline of the smallish leaves that gives them a lacy, completely delightful effect regardless of their color. This, combined with the spreading, rounded, sometimes mound-like character of the tree as a whole, puts it in a class by itself for single-specimen planting in situations where an eye-catching but not overwhelming accent is needed. For example, I have seen it used to excellent advantage on either side of a broad driveway entrance; at the end of a straight garden path, at the top of a flight of garden steps to increase their apparent drop, or at the bottom to minimize it; and to fill an "empty" corner at the edge of a lawn where a regular tree would be too tall and a mixed shrub planting too lacking in unity.

220

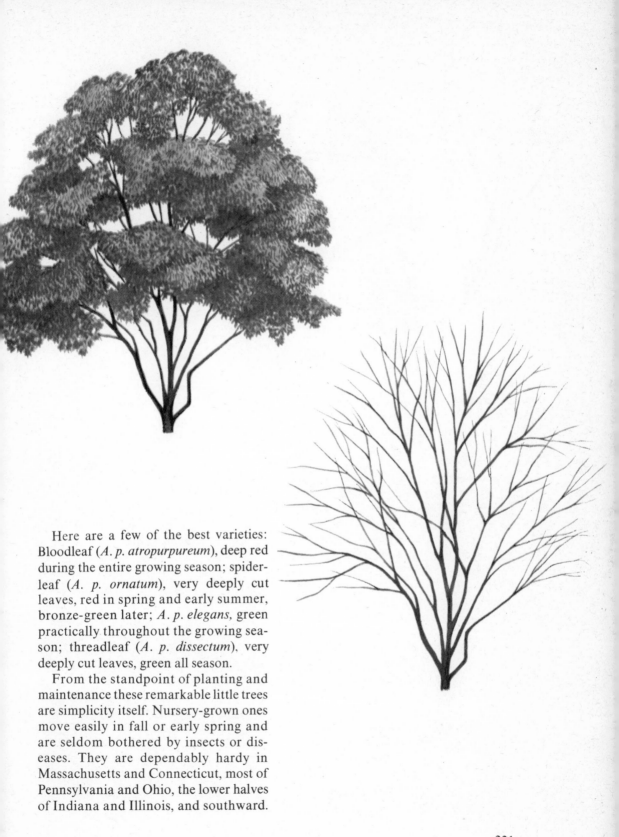

Here are a few of the best varieties: Bloodleaf (*A. p. atropurpureum*), deep red during the entire growing season; spider-leaf (*A. p. ornatum*), very deeply cut leaves, red in spring and early summer, bronze-green later; *A. p. elegans*, green practically throughout the growing season; threadleaf (*A. p. dissectum*), very deeply cut leaves, green all season.

From the standpoint of planting and maintenance these remarkable little trees are simplicity itself. Nursery-grown ones move easily in fall or early spring and are seldom bothered by insects or diseases. They are dependably hardy in Massachusetts and Connecticut, most of Pennsylvania and Ohio, the lower halves of Indiana and Illinois, and southward.

221

WHITE PINE
(*Pinus strobus*)

If you are thinking of a large, exceptionally handsome evergreen tree for planting as a single background specimen or perhaps a group to ward off the worst of winter's winds, be sure to consider the white pine. Since the first settlers landed on the New England coast this has been hailed as one of America's outstanding trees. Today, although its once vast forests have vanished before the lumberman's ax, its ornamental rating is higher than ever.

The natural range of white pines covers an immense territory that extends from Newfoundland to Lake Winnipeg, through the upper Midwest, down through New England to central New Jersey, and southward among the Alleghenies as far as northern Georgia. It will do well beyond these limits, too, if planted in the right sort of place and kept regularly and freely watered for at least the first full year.

Its single trunk is tall and straight unless, as happened to the old fellow in our illustration, some accident forces it to fork and develop a strikingly picturesque form. Its masses of slender, flexible, bluish-green needles toss and roll in the wind like living waves.

White pine naturally grows to be a big tree—50 to 75 feet tall, and occasionally twice the latter height. However, it is easier to restrict by pruning than others. The secret of success in early midsummer trimming is to cut the twigs only in the middle of those portions that carry needles, never farther back where the bark is bare of them. Another successful technique is to shorten the "candles" of new growth when they are well grown but before their needles appear.

Any kind of good, well-drained soil suits white pines. They are easily transplanted while small and when well established may grow 10 feet in 10 years.

CANADA HEMLOCK
(*Tsuga canadensis*)

To say that the Canada hemlock is one of the two finest evergreen trees in the Northeastern states sounds like a strong statement, but I've been saying it for a good many years. The hemlock's only rival for the top honor is that other native American, the white pine.

This densely branched and needled conifer can stand almost any amount of cold weather without the slightest effect on its remarkable feathery appearance. It's a cool-country tree. You can grow it as a gracefully tapered, broad spire with a mast-straight trunk, or shear it so as to form a tall hedge so dense that even a cat would have trouble getting through it. Or a group of several unpruned ones in a corner of a large property will create a North Country effect.

Hemlocks dislike windy places, and develop their most perfect form where they have some protection from the worst winter blasts.

Hemlocks are neat trees with slender, supple branches, pliant twigs, and short, flattened needles, the undersides paler and more silvery than the rich, glossy green of the upper surface. Even the cones are hardly larger than elongated light brown buttons.

Well-formed young trees up to 3 or 4 feet high can be readily transplanted from the wild in early spring if their rather straggly roots are taken up practically intact and kept moist. All evergreens should be well watered for the first full year.

A hemlock is not an especially deep-rooted tree, and it will grow almost as well on a rocky hillside as in a level place. Although it stands a reasonable amount of dry weather, it needs a fair supply of soil moisture and sometimes grows in cold swamps that are not constantly waterlogged.

223

GRAY BIRCH
(*Betula populifolia*)

There are two schools of thought concerning the gray birch. Out in the back country the farm folk consider it a "weed tree," because thickets of it often spring up in abandoned fields and dry wastelands with the enthusiasm of dandelions. But in many a suburb and small residential town throughout New England, New York, and southward through Delaware, its rating is very different. There, homeowners value it for its grace, the beauty of its bright green leaves, which dance so prettily in every passing breeze, and the unique yet harmonious note that its form and coloring bring to virtually any landscaping scheme. The true white birch is another tree, larger, rarer, and also fine.

All the birches are essentially tallish trees with numerous slender branches and distinctive bark. Even more distinctive is the gray birch's habit of producing several full-size trunks from the same crown, as shown in the illustration. In time each of these may reach a height of 30 feet, forming a lawn or background clump that is outstandingly beautiful.

There is no trick about growing the gray birch well, for it accepts practically any soil and exposure provided there is plenty of sunlight. For best development it should be well away from other trees, for if crowded there will be a tendency for many of the smaller lower branches to develop poorly and eventually die.

Lawn grass grows well under it, for its

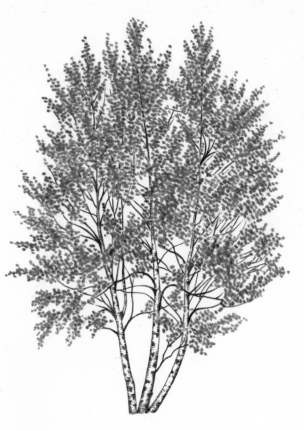

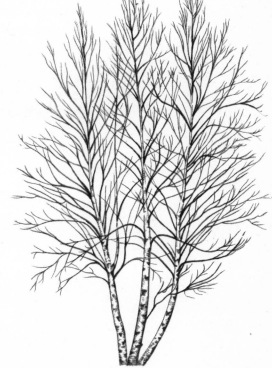

root system is neither large nor thirsty.

In early spring, when most of the plant world is starting its first strong growth, the gray birch is delicately shrouded in a pale green mist as countless slender catkins deck its twigs like tinsel on a Christmas tree. Soon the effect gains strength with the opening of the almost triangular leaves. All summer long their vivid green is a delight that will hardly be lessened even when the color lightens and then yellows with the autumn.

In some local areas the warm-weather loveliness of gray birches may be marred by one of plant life's smaller enemies, a tiny sawfly whose larvae tunnel inside the leaves. Spraying in late May will catch these leaf miners.

225

AMERICAN ELM
(*Ulmus americana*)

From New England to the Rockies, and southward as far as Florida and Texas, the American Elm is hailed as a model of stateliness and well-bred grace. In maturity its finest form is vaselike. Only in ripe old age do its outward-trending limbs lose their perfectly graduated taper and become a trifle portly. Before this becomes noticeable the tree may be 80 or 100 feet tall, which certainly entitles it to carry a bit of extra weight!

As a home-grounds shade tree this famous elm has certain unique advantages. One is its high-branching habit, which enables it to shade the roof of a nearby house without shutting off too much breeze or light at the window levels, or from the lawn.

To dyed-in-the-wool gardeners, however, the elm's special habit of underground growth has its disadvantages. A big one thinks nothing of laying a network of tough, whiplike, and ever-hungry feeding roots only a foot or so below the surface of a laboriously prepared flower or vegetable garden many yards beyond the limits of the tree's branch spread.

American elms can be grown almost anywhere in reasonably rich and moist soil. They grow rather rapidly, and their strongly patterned and rather stiff leaves, their almost geometrical veining showing clearly in the accompanying detail drawing, are a rich and thoroughly satisfying green throughout the summer.

One of the elm's shortcomings is its susceptibility to attack by the elm leaf beetle, which may skeletonize the foliage. There is one remedy for it: a thorough spraying with arsenate of lead in mid-spring.

Another potential problem is the Dutch elm disease, which is carried from tree to tree by a small bark beetle. Some years ago it was feared that this serious ailment would destroy the bulk of New England's famous elms. But today there is hope that it won't spread westward and that it can be controlled.

226

227

SUGAR MAPLE
(*Acer saccharum*)

Few indeed are the trees that hold top rating for shade and form, magnificent autumn coloring, and a variety of subtly flavored sweets with country-wide fame. Only in the sugar maple are all these assets achieved. It is not the only maple species that has sap used for syrup and sugar making, but it is the best. Sugar maples are cool-country trees, growing wild in well-drained places from southern Newfoundland west along the St. Lawrence River to the Great Lakes and southward through the Appalachian system to northern Georgia and eastern Texas. The Great Lakes region produces the biggest ones—over 100 feet in height, with a 5-foot trunk diameter.

A sugar maple grows more slowly than most others of its race. Its numerous long branches have a definitely upward rather than horizontal trend. Thus it becomes a dense, broad-topped, and well-balanced dome that casts ample shade without blanketing too much lawn space. The wood is hard and springy and the tree's whole framework seems designed to weather both wind and ice storms.

If you have a coolish climate this outstanding tree has many home-ground uses. It is perfect for property-line plantings, and how often a fine old specimen shades a little farmhouse without shutting out the wandering breeze. It has great merit as a background specimen and will cast a long, broad shadow across the lawn in the late hours of a sultry

summer afternoon. Everyone knows how beautiful it is in autumn—a red, gold, and brown climax to a long green summer.

Assuming that you obtain your sugar maple from a first-class nursery where it has been properly grown, there is small likelihood that it will need any pruning for many years. If any cutting should become necessary, do it *in summer* so as to avoid "bleeding."

I wish it were possible to promise that your sugar maple will cap its career with yielding a generous supply of home-grown syrup or sugar. But it takes anywhere from fifty to a hundred gallons of sap to make a single gallon of syrup. So you'd need a grove of maples to sweeten your breakfast pancakes for a season.

WHITE OAK
(Quercus alba)

The white oak comes as close to being the perfect large shade tree as any species in America. It has a deep-striking root system that permits a good turf of shade-tolerant lawn grass right up to the base of its trunk.

A white oak is a year-round tree. In winter you never tire of its splendidly proportioned gray frame, which will be so marvelously tinted with a soft pink veil as the myriad leaf buds start to open in the spring. Then, as the days grow warmer, there will be the expanding canopy of bright olive-green leaves with their paler undersides, ornamented for a

time in May or June with countless slender catkins hanging like long yellowish pendants from every twig, and when summer comes, and until autumn turns the green to purplish red, you will enjoy the perfect sunshade of the full-grown big leaves, many of which cling to their twigs well into the winter.

On the practical side white oaks are notably resistant to serious breakage by wind or ice storms, and their branch pattern is such that electric and telephone wires can be carried safely through with little or no unsightly pruning to mar the handsome outlines.

The white oak grows too big for most small lots, yet if you are so fortunate as to have a fine white oak already on your place, don't ever let anyone persuade you to part with it!

As with most kinds of shade and ornamental trees, white oaks should be bought from first-class nurseries where they have been grown for shape and root-pruned in order to develop root structures favorable to transplanting. If you should decide to collect a seedling from some nearby field or woods, better not try one more than two feet tall, and be sure to get *all* of its deep taproot.

SHAGBARK HICKORY
(*Carya ovata*)

No one could fairly call the shagbark hickory beautiful. It is a little on the rough-diamond side, with strong, often ungainly limbs that seem to have a variety of individual ideas on where or how to grow, coupled with a determination to carry them out. If shagbarks were human they would probably wear farm overalls and cowhide boots, and be perfectly at home in them. And when the weather got rough they would keep plugging right along with all the hardiness that is built into their tough, enduring bodies.

Yet it does have its moods of loveliness. There are surprising tones of subtle color when bright sunlight strikes across the curved, pale brown-gray slabs of loosened bark that give the tree its popular name. And a quite different note of quiet expectancy is struck as spring starts the buffy green coats of the twig-tip buds to swelling larger and larger until, suddenly, they pop open under the pressure of baby leaves often accompanied by pendant catkins of surprising delicacy and charm. Within a week or two this phase vanishes under the rising tide of the tree's life cycle, but you are sure to recall it months later as you notice the ripening nuts that are one of the shagbark's major achievements.

As you may have guessed, shagbarks become big trees—often 60 to 80 feet tall. They are adaptable fellows, too, provided you give them an abundance

232

of rich, well-drained soil and an open location only moderately sloping.

No hickory species is easy to transplant when of any size, for its first major step in life is to send a sturdy taproot as far and straight down into the ground as possible. A nut-tree specialist can sell you one of a selected strain. Finding wild seedings is difficult; they're hard to identify. Planting a few top-quality nuts, screened to keep hungry mice and squirrels away, will work if you're patient.

WEEPING WILLOW
(*Salix babylonica*)

Among all the 300-odd members of its tribe the weeping or Babylonia willow is the most widely known for its unique value as a landscape tree. Only the pussy-willows, prime favorites of millions who welcome the early foretastes of spring, can match it in popularity.

A typical weeping willow reaches its full height of 30 or 40 feet rather rapidly, for it has the family trait of surprisingly speedy growth. It is always the epitome of well-bred grace, touched at times with quiet laughter as though the tree thoroughly enjoyed just being alive.

The weeping willow's best season starts with the spring appearance of countless slender, pointed 6-inch leaves strung along the hanging and almost cordlike branchlets. All through the summer and well into autumn the clean, living veil casts luminous yet grateful shade, perfect for dreamy lounging. If there is a cool spot to be found, it will be here.

Such a tree is clearly one for single-specimen use, for if it were sandwiched in among others its effectiveness would surely be compromised. Since it needs no underplanting and its roots are spread widely it can, if you wish, be provided with informal outdoor furniture to be used for comfortable alfresco meals or lounging. Even an uncemented flagged or pebbled terrace around the base may not be amiss.

There are actually several different kinds of good pendulous willow trees. Farther north—let's say in the upper two thirds of the United States—the leading weeping species is the golden willow, which is much hardier and quite similar in character. There are also a few hybrid forms containing a good deal of babylonica "blood," their hardiness lying between that of the golden and its cousin. The chief need is that its roots shall be able to get water, which they have an uncanny ability to find if it is anywhere around.

CALIFORNIA BUCKEYE
(Aesculus californica)

Botanically speaking, a buckeye is a horse chestnut. It is a native Californian, but it has been planted as an ornamental in several other parts of the world and deserves to be better known in others.

It isn't a big tree, as such things go, for its maximum height is around 40 feet. But it is broad and densely branched, as the illustrations show. It is essentially a tree for mild climates, for it simply cannot stand genuine cold.

When the gracefully pointed leaflets are well grown, the flowers come, white or light rose in color, rather picturesquely formed, and massed in roughly cylindrical sprays that curve gracefully. And every one of them is out in the open where it can be seen to best advantage.

Then, in summer, you will begin to notice the development of the 2-inch nuts, each in its thin-skinned green case that yellows slightly as the days of maturity approach. In all the world I know of no nut as intriguing as a well-ripened buckeye. On one side, where the base of the husk has been, there is a round, pale area like the pupil of a great eye in reverse—the obvious origin of the name buckeye, or buck's eye.

The buckeye's disadvantage? It litters the ground with flowers and nuts. And you cannot eat the nuts.

237

GORDONIA
(*Gordonia alatamaha*)

The time to see a gordonia at the peak of its effectiveness is late August and September. During this season its rather loose but upright figure is casually starred with white, cuplike blossoms nearly 3 inches across in a setting of long, shining leaves, colors ranging from deep green to scarlet. Whether its height be 10 feet or 25, it presents a picture unmatched by any other species, particularly at a time of year when flowers on woody plants are rare indeed.

Some gordonias have multiple trunks and grow like tall shrubs, while others have a well-defined tree form. Their best landscaping use is in spots where they can be seen at close range, for at a distance much of their unique beauty is lost. A situation near the house or beside a much-used garden path is often ideal.

Few American trees have a history as strange and puzzling as the gordonia's. It was discovered somewhere in the valley of the Altamaha River, northern Georgia, in the year 1765, by John Bartram, the famous plant hunter. It is believed that all the trees currently in cultivation trace their ancestry back to a single specimen, now dead, that Bartram planted in his Philadelphia garden about 1778. He named it Franklinia, for Benjamin Franklin, but gordonia is the most-used name. Through the years that intervened between 1800 and the present time many individuals and expeditions have combed the Altamaha River country without finding a single wild gordonia. So far as we know the last time one was seen in its native haunts was in 1790. It is sometimes called the Lost Tree.

239

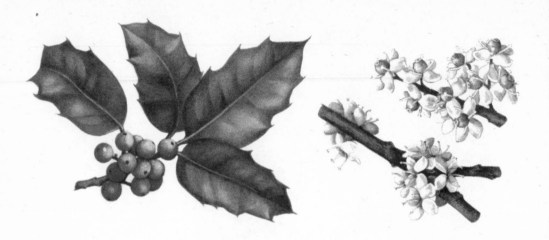

AMERICAN HOLLY
(*Ilex opaca*)

American holly is probably the most famous of America's broad-leaved evergreen trees, and, as far as most homeowners are concerned, the least understood with respect to its culture and fruiting requirements. Most people have little conception of its ability to withstand winter cold, or of the fact that it is a unisexual species—that is, any given one is either all male or all female. Only the females produce berries, and this only after their tiny blossoms have been fertilized with pollen from the flowers of a male. Fortunately two simple and sure cures for this are available: (1) plant a female in the preferred display location and a male nearby; (2) buy a female on which a male branch has been inconspicuously grafted.

Originally the American holly grew wild from coastal Massachusetts to Florida and inland to Texas. Thorough research by growers has demonstrated rather conclusively that hollies vary greatly in hardiness, and it is now possible to purchase specimens that not only have superior foliage, form, and fruit, but are surprisingly resistant to northern winter climates. More than 75 varieties of American holly are known.

X

THE GARDEN CLUB STORY

by Helen S. Hull

"More grows in the garden than the gardener sows."
OLD SPANISH PROVERB

BETTY HULETT, APSA

The Lincoln Memorial Garden in Illinois is a special project of the state federation of garden clubs.

GARDEN clubs are as American as the proverbial apple pie. But unlike that delectable dish, gardening is organized nowhere else in the world as in the three national garden club organizations in the United States—the National Council of State Garden Clubs, the Garden Club of America, and Men's Garden Clubs of America. There are other organizations, such as the Women's National Farm and Garden Association, allied to the garden club idea, but they are not included in this story.

ORIGIN OF GARDEN CLUBS   How did it all start, and how has it prospered? More than sixty years ago garden clubs began springing up in cities and towns. They had their earliest beginning in an individual interest in growing things for pleasure, and the inevitable American desire to share the pleasure and knowledge gained with kindred souls of one's own neighborhood. Perhaps even in those early days the motivation was not too far from that of today. Today perhaps someone has just moved into a new house and wants to grow a few flowers for color at the front door, or in a window box. What is the best way to do it? The housewife sees her neighbor has a colorful bed of petunias that gives a most pleasing effect. What seed did she use? How did she prepare the soil? How can the effect be equaled in her own yard? She has

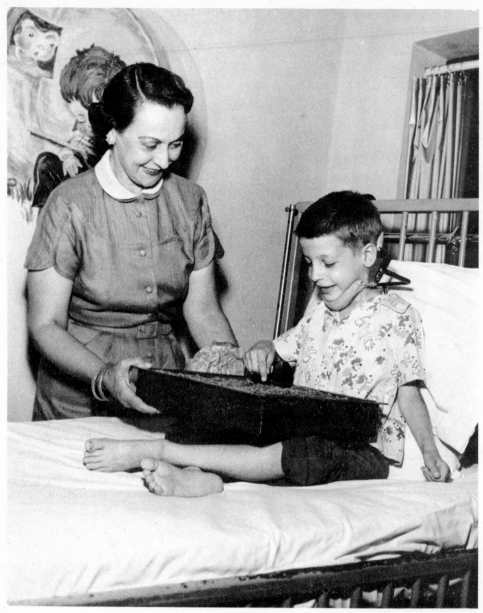

This is garden therapy, a major civic project of many state garden clubs. Six-year-old Larry Glockzin plants rye seed in a pan of sifted sphagnum moss under the direction of Mrs. Leslie Stratton of the Belle Fleur Garden Club of Waco. Veterans' hospitals, a prison farm, corrective schools, institutions for the blind and for crippled children are among the places where the Texas Garden Clubs, Inc., have projects. The National Council chairman of garden therapy is Mrs. John Berry of Goldthwaite, Texas.

a friend down the street who also would like to know some of these things, and before you can say Jack Robinson, they have their heads together and another garden club is born.

There were hundreds of garden clubs in local communities for many years before the great state and national organizations were formed. Although the basic idea was to share and improve gardening knowledge and pleasure, the clubs early took on responsibility for beautification of the community surroundings, such as schools, hospitals, and the town parks. From this local civic interest grew a desire to take part in the solution of state and national problems affecting gardening, horticulture, and civic beautification. As early as 1930 the *Garden Club of America History* recounts, "When the garden club train stopped at Calgary on its way west, two farmers were heard discussing the delegation with much curiosity. One suggested Gold Star Mothers, but the other who knew said, 'Nothing like 'em, them's lady gardeners.' 'And what might they be doing?' 'Nothing much, just going around *trying to beautify the world.*'" It is in civic duty that the garden clubs of the United States have developed in a way to set them apart from gardening organizations anywhere else in the world, and this partly answers the question of their phenomenal growth.

Although there are groups that bear the name of garden clubs in other countries, they would not be recognized as such in the United States. In France the "garden club" is composed of the owners of large estates, about 150 in all of France, who visit each other. Some Americans in France were interested in starting garden clubs there that could be participated in by the owners of modest homes and average means, but so far nothing has been heard from this endeavor. In England and in the Commonwealth horticultural societies are the nearest approach to garden clubs. A former president of the Garden Club of New Jersey now living in Durban, South Africa, writes: "Though I have tried, and am trying still, garden clubs are just not wanted in South Africa." There are garden clubs, however, affiliated with the American organizations, in Puerto Rico, Hawaii, Alaska, Montreal, Toronto, and Bermuda and an unaffiliated one in Mexico City.

The National Council of State Garden Clubs is by far the largest national organization, embracing more than 310,000 members in 10,000 community garden clubs, which in turn are members of 43 state garden club federations. One of the aims of the National Council is to encourage more and more gardeners in every community.

To be a member, it is necessary only to belong to a garden club acceptable as a member of the state garden club federation, which pays the 10¢ per capita dues to the national organization. With this policy the National Council, since its organization in 1929, has shown an increase in member-

The Founders Memorial Garden, on the campus of the University of Georgia, is a joint project of the Garden Club of Georgia and the university's landscape department, honoring the twelve founders of the Ladies Garden Club of Athens, first American garden club.

ship of as many as 50,000 members in a single year. It now stands more than ten times larger than any other gardening organization in the world.

The Garden Club of America, organized in 1913, with a policy of more selective membership, is patterned on a regional rather than a state federation basis. It now has dues of $5.00 per capita and is composed of 268 clubs with a total membership of 10,000. Many of the clubs that are members of the Garden Club of America belong also to their state garden club federation and are thus also members of the National Council.

Although these two national garden club organizations are predominantly comprised of women, they do not exclude men. There are an estimated 10,000 male members in the National Council, either through garden clubs exclusively of men, or in clubs to which both husband and wife belong. Twenty-seven times men have served as presidents of state garden club federations and the National Council board of directors has included men in all of the twenty-five years of its existence.

246

The Men's Garden Clubs of America put on educational displays like this at the New York Flower Show. Roses, vegetables, dahlias, chrysanthemums, and greenhouse gardening, as well as test garden projects, are among the special interests of the 7000 members.

Either through "insurrection" or through inevitable development the Men's Garden Clubs of America came into its own in 1932 with the slogan "More pants in the garden." Today the Men's Garden Clubs of America, with dues of $1.00 per member, has grown to 7000 in 176 member clubs in 30 states. The men claim, and the women concede, that there is a higher percentage of expert gardeners among the members of the Men's Garden Clubs. Or at least they work at it more exclusively! Although there are exceptions, in the main they refuse to be diverted by other activities that command the attention of the women, such as conservation and civic beautification. Their national program includes "test gardens" throughout the country, where new varieties of plants are grown in order to evaluate their usefulness and suitability in various situations of climate. At flower shows the exhibits of the Men's Garden Clubs are always most practical and useful demonstrations of gardening practice, and this year their exhibit won the highest award at the International Flower Show in New York. A press reporter remarked of their

247

LEFT: After World War II the National Council brought states and garden clubs into the Blue Star Memorial Highway project. RIGHT: Highway plantings and roadside development are constant projects on 16,000 miles of highways, reaching every state.

annual convention that he had never seen a convention with "so many pipes and so few bottles." Their hearty approach to gardening, and their enjoyment of it, is leaven to gardening development in the United States.

These three national gardening associations are incorporated as educational, non-profit organizations and, except for actual expenses of administration, all work is on a volunteer basis. Although the membership includes top experts in every field of gardening and horticulture, participation in the work of garden clubs is amateur in the classic meaning of the word, that is, from devotion to it. In fact the National Council has a rule that officers and members of its board of directors may not remain on the board and accept pay for any services performed in connection with their garden club duties.

What is the cause of this devotion? What is the pull that has enrolled hundreds of thousands of members in the garden clubs? What do the garden clubs do that enlists such interest and such loyalty? Is it the art of gardening alone? Is it social? Is it civic duty? The answer is complex. From the inception of the first garden clubs "civic duty" has been a part of the concept expressed in the early clubs in flower and vegetable shows to which the public was invited and often participated.

The concern in community betterment now takes form in numerous garden club committees, local, state, and national, to initiate and carry

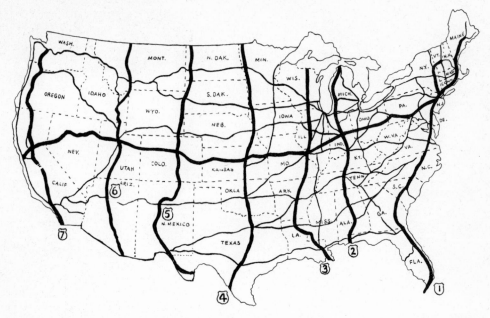

Blue Star Memorial Highways cover all of the forty-eight states.

through civic beautification projects. Every once in a while some members complain that gardening and horticulture are now the stepchildren of the garden clubs, that civic betterment is the major interest. Committees to promote conservation, garden centers, junior gardening, roadside protection and development, garden therapy, and flower show schools are a part of every state federation program and that of the National Council.

But at the local garden club level gardening is being taught more earnestly today than ever before. Everyone who has a home now wants a garden, and since the great part of today's gardening, like today's cooking, is done without benefit of skilled help, the homeowners are learning how to have the garden they want through belonging to garden clubs. If there isn't one in the community they form one, and either pool their gardening experiences for mutual benefit or engage lecturers on garden subjects for their club meetings.

The Men's Garden Clubs have never been lured from the gardening path to wage battles against the billboards or to fight for preservation of our natural heritage of beauty, such as "Save the Redwoods." The garden clubs of the National Council and of the Garden Club of America are militant leaders in developing enlightened opinion in these matters of public concern and other questions, such as conservation of water, forests, and all renewable

Littered scenes like this in Washington inspired "Don't Be a Litterbug" campaign.

national resources. They have well-organized committees to advance both projects and education in these fields. Furthermore their numbers are now so great that politicians must listen to what the garden clubs advocate whether they choose to do so or not.

Politics as such, that is, partisan politics, are never mentioned and have no part in the internal organization of garden clubs or in their public advocacy. Participation by the garden clubs is strictly non-partisan on questions that concern the welfare of America. They advocate the preservation and development of the national parks and forests, so that the national heritage of beauty can be enjoyed by present and future generations of all the people. They urge that the national parks shall be adequately staffed and kept clean and that no part of them shall be invaded for civic expediency or for commercial or political interests. They strive to raise the national level of

250

Girl Scouts, National Council, and local groups work together for clean roadsides.

good taste through campaigns against litter and to instill a sense of obligation in every citizen toward maintaining neatness and cleanliness in public parks and along roadsides. The National Council's "Don't Be a Litterbug" campaign is catching on throughout the country. This attitude of the garden clubs against public untidiness exists not only because billboards and other roadside blights and litter are ugly, but because they believe that how America looks both reflects and conditions how America thinks.

The garden clubs are deeply patriotic, although there is no flag-waving to proclaim it. In the past there have been attempts to formalize state and national meetings and procedures to make the garden clubs full of pomp and circumstance, like some other national women's organizations. These attempts, however, have passed out of style and, except for a simple identification pin available to be purchased by garden club presidents, there are no insignia

251

Flower show schools are a major project of National Council. Here Mrs. W. H. Wilson teaches color harmonies in the Dallas course. Each year more than 16,000 members attend such classes.

whatever. Garden club members are a starry-eyed band, but as practical as the old shoes in which they garden.

GARDEN TOURS AND PILGRIMAGES   Members go to the state and national meetings in order to attend to the business at hand and to meet people and to see different parts of the United States under circumstances they could not duplicate in any other way. "Join the Navy and see the world" is also applicable to the garden clubs—"Join the garden clubs and see the world." The *Garden Club of America History* further recounts a fictitious but amusing story that illustrates how eagerly delegates attend the national conventions. "One enthusiast regretfully wired that her husband's illness would prevent her going to the annual meeting, then wired that he was better and she could go, then wired that he was worse, then that he had died and she could go after all. The lure of the annual meeting could go no further."

State and national meetings are often followed by tours of homes and gardens and historic sites of nearby areas; but also garden club pilgrimages have extended outside the United States. As many as three or four hundred at a time on chartered boats and planes have visited Europe, Hawaii, Mexico, Bermuda, Alaska, Japan, and the National Council even held a national meeting across the Canadian border in Montreal.

Not all of these tours and pilgrimages are enjoyed by garden club members alone. They may be organized by garden clubs and be made available to

252

CHARLES R. PEARSON   AL MONNER, PORTLAND, OREGON

The Garden Club of New Jersey first exhibited the now famous Peace rose. At right conventioning garden club members from the National Council see Mt. Hood.

the public for a fee as a means to raise funds for civic projects. Several of the pilgrimages originated by the garden clubs have become nationally and even world famous. The Natchez, Mississippi, tours of ante-bellum homes and historic sites now attract more than 50,000 tourists every year during the month of March. The origin of the Natchez tours is a case of an ill wind blowing good. The local garden clubs were to entertain garden clubs from other parts of the state in a tour of Natchez gardens. That year, however, a frost destroyed the camellias and the Natchez garden club members were in despair, since, when the time came, they had no gardens to show. Instead they polished the old silver, dusted the old china; they ransacked their grandmothers' trunks, and donned the colonial costumes. They dressed up the children in pantalets and their mammies with white aprons and colored kerchiefs, and all waited to welcome the visitors. The tour was such a success that they repeated it the following year for a fee and out of this has grown the Natchez tour as it is today. To give an idea of the proportions of such an enterprise, in one year more than $50,000 was paid the government in admissions taxes. The profits from this garden club project are used to restore historic buildings and a portion is given the owners of the homes on display to keep them refurbished in ante-bellum style.

Garden pilgrimages have grown throughout the garden club world in many states. And they have become a major vacation objective of thousands of American families. State and local chambers of commerce see the value in

253

A demonstration of the Pennsylvania Horticultural Society shows a haphazard way, and a better, planned way, to use the same flowers in a home arrangement.

these tours and heartily co-operate in advertising them. South Carolina, Virginia, Maryland, Pennsylvania, Colorado, and Texas have notably successful yearly tours. A tour notice in the *National Gardener,* the publication of the National Council of State Garden Clubs, brought to the state chamber of commerce in Georgia five hundred inquiries for information regarding the Georgia tour from all over the United States.

MEMORIAL GARDENS   In some instances the profit from the tour of houses and gardens is used to establish memorial gardens, the most notable of which is the Lincoln Memorial Garden in Springfield, Illinois. This living memorial to the Great Emancipator was initiated by the local garden club of Springfield. The project was soon adopted by the state federation of garden clubs, the Garden Club of Illinois, and the first plantings were made in 1936. More than one hundred garden clubs of Illinois and several state federations and the National Council have made plantings or otherwise contributed to this project. After completion of the planting of the sixty-acre tract the garden club turned the memorial over to the city, but the garden club maintains its interest and the city cannot change the plans without the consent of the garden club. The sixty acres are planted with wild flowers, shrubs, and trees native to Illinois, and in the simple, rustic manner that suggests everywhere in the garden, "where Lincoln walked." Annual tours now attracting national

The Municipal Rose Garden in Tulsa, Oklahoma, was established in 1935 by the Tulsa Garden Club. Formal in design, it covers six acres and has more than 12,000 rose plants.

interest of gardens and Lincoln shrines furnish funds for the perpetuation of this lovely garden.

The Garden Club of Georgia, in co-operation with the Landscape Architecture Department of the University of Georgia, has sponsored a memorial garden on the campus of the University of Athens, honoring the twelve founders of the Ladies Garden Club of Athens, Georgia, founded in 1891 and reputed to be the first garden club as we know them today. This club is still existent, as is the even earlier Cambridge Plant Club, founded in 1889.

Another memorial that is growing in significance is the Garden Club of New Jersey Arboretum, Nell Baker Saunders Memorial, established in Greenbrook Sanctuary in Interstate Park on top of the Palisades overlooking the Hudson River. The rugged area is being planted with shrubs, trees, and flowers native to this historic area, with emphasis upon plants that are attractive to birds, for the Arboretum is also a bird and wild-life sanctuary. The state organization raised $11,000 for initial plantings, and individual clubs are adding small plantings for "Fern Trail," "Dogwood Trail," "Azalea Trail," and others. The state clubs donated funds also for a large pavilion within the Arboretum for meetings and shelter, and hopes someday to expand this into a trailside museum. The number of memorial gardens, large and small, throughout the United States planted and maintained by the garden clubs can hardly be estimated.

BLUE STAR MEMORIAL HIGHWAY   The largest and most ambitious of all "memorial gardens" is the "Blue Star Memorial Highway," now comprising 16,000 miles of legally memorialized highways, as a "Living Tribute to this nation's Armed Forces—to the men and women who have, or will serve that we might continue to live in freedom and peace in America the Beautiful." This project was originated by the Garden Club of New Jersey in 1944 as the Blue Star Drive, a five-mile strip of highway between Mountainside and North Plainfield, to be planted with flowering dogwood trees as a pledge to the men and women then serving in the Armed Forces of World War II. The New Jersey garden clubs raised $25,000 for the purchase of trees, and the State Highway Department co-operated in planting and maintaining the plantings along the route. Ten years ago, at the dedication of Blue Star Drive, the garden clubs made a pledge they strive to keep: "Blue Star Drive, then, may be a significant symbol not only of love and gratitude, but of that responsibility which we should acknowledge and assume. We all know that no matter how decisive the battle on foreign fields, the better world for which they fight, the real and lasting victory must be won here at home in every hamlet, town and state in this nation. Let Blue Star Drive be the pledge of our determination not to quit the battle until the real victory is won."

In 1945 the National Council adopted the Blue Star Memorial as a national project and the state federations through state legislatures have memorialized routes in forty-one states, so that the Blue Star Highway extends

The Garden Club of America exhibit at the 1954 New York Flower Show deserved high praise. Inside the replica of a colonial captain's house were demonstrations of flower arrangements. On each side were Early American types of gardens, like that of the Salt Box House below.

PHOTOGRAPHS: JOHN HUGELMEYER, NEW YORK

Glass house, precursor of today's home greenhouses, was exhibited by the Providence Garden Club and Garden Club of America. Below, an Early American keeping room, set up by Rhode Island garden clubs: Little Compton, Newport, South County, and Bennington.

PHOTOGRAPHS: JOHN HUGELMEYER, NEW YORK

not only from coast to coast on U. S. Route 40, but from Maine to Florida, principally on Route 1, and with laterals through every state connecting the Blue Star Routes, roadsides now under the protection of the state garden clubs in co-operation with their state highway departments. Blue Star markers are being purchased and erected by the garden clubs, and suitable plantings featuring either the "state tree," or one chosen by the garden club as the most beautiful flowering tree of that state.

The American Association of Nurserymen co-operated with the project in furnishing a planting design suitable for the areas around the memorial markers, and nurserymen have co-operated in donating plantings or giving special rates for the purchase of the flowering trees. In New Jersey more than 10,000 flowering dogwoods have been planted on the original strip, and now the project has been extended across the state, under the protection of the Blue Star Highway Council, appointed by the governor.

At the same time the garden clubs are working for protection of all highways through planning, zoning, and safety legislation that can eventually stop the despoliation of our public highways by commercial blights, especially billboards. It is the contention of the garden clubs that the roadside rights of way and the view, as well as the concrete roadbed, belong to the public, which pays for them, and should not be appropriated by billboards that are ugly and, by their purpose of attention-getting, create safety hazards. "Don't buy products advertised on billboards" was one of the earliest slogans of the garden clubs, occurring as early as 1915. Elimination of billboards has not been among their most successful aims, but garden clubs believe they are making headway in apprising the public of rights and attitudes toward these matters. Some industrialists have seen the light in their responsibility to the welfare of all by refusing to use this medium for their advertising.

GIFTS TO THE PUBLIC   The garden clubs are not always raising funds, memorializing, or on a militant crusade. One of the most famous public rose gardens was donated to the city by the Tulsa Garden Club in 1935, covering six acres and including more than 12,000 rose plants. Such gardens, in greater or less degree, dot the map of the United States. Through contributions of members the Garden Club of America donated $85,000 for the purchase of redwood groves in California along the Redwood Highway. Their donations purchased for posterity 2556 acres in 1930. In 1949 the National Council donated $8000, purchasing two groves of forty acres each, as their "Twentieth Anniversary Gift to the Nation." That same year the California Garden Clubs donated $5000 for the purchase of another forty acres of these historic trees to preserve their majestic beauty for future generations.

Conservation projects sponsored by individual clubs are being developed in every state. The Garden Club of America donates its "Founders Fund" of $1200 each year to the project in conservation voted the most worthy of any proposed by its member clubs.

SCHOLARSHIPS   In addition to conservation projects funds are contributed yearly for scholarships to young people who wish to study horticulture or landscape architecture either as undergraduates or at the fellowship level. The National Council has set aside $40,000 for scholarship uses. The Garden Club of America has an endowment fellowship fund of $50,000 for use at the American Academy of Landscape Architecture in Rome. This organization has made sizable contributions for plantings at many established horticultural enterprises, such as at the National Arboretum in Washington, D. C.

GARDEN CENTERS   Funds for establishment of garden centers in all parts of the United States have been raised or donated by garden clubs, as their gift to their communities, so that through the garden center, horticultural activities and information are available to everyone in the community. "The real purpose of a Garden Center is to provide a link between members of garden clubs, potential gardeners and the general public in order to increase knowledge of horticulture, conservation and civic beautification. A garden center serves as a source of free gardening information and is constantly working for the advancement of horticultural practices and the improvement of home and civic landscape. You don't have to be a garden club member to benefit by its activities. There is no social barrier connected with the operation of such a center, for it is created to serve all gardeners who wish to use its services."

The Cleveland Garden Center not only has a fine building, but an expert staff, and has been in operation since 1930. The Jacksonville, Florida, Garden Club has established a garden center in a building they have built for the purpose at a cost of over $50,000. Abilene, Texas, has just spent $32,000 for their garden center building. The Berkshire Garden Center, at Stockbridge, Massachusetts, supported by the garden clubs of the area, has become a center of interest for travelers to the Berkshire Music Festival. They visit the experimental gardens and model plantings on the grounds and avail themselves of the advice on gardening, always free for the asking from the horticulturists in charge. The Garden Club of Georgia reports twenty-two garden centers within that one state established by the member garden clubs,

The Garden Club of America award, the Fenwick Medal, was won by this arrangement of orchid leaves and silver tree blossoms, created by Mrs. Irving M. Day at the New York International Flower Show in 1954.   JOHN HUGELMEYER, NEW YORK

260

and all in all there are more than seven hundred throughout the United States maintained by garden clubs. In smaller communities the garden center may be a shelf of garden books in the town library.

FLOWER SHOWS Another service to the public is through more than 8000 flower shows given by garden clubs every year, which the public may attend. In order to make these shows of higher and higher quality in both horticulture and artistic use of flowers the National Council conducts its Flower Show Schools, which more than 16,000 members attend every year. These schools instruct in how to put on a flower show, how to grow specimen flowers, how to make flower arrangements, how to use flowers in the home, how to stage educational exhibits. Through the courses of study, and examinations supplemented by required reading in all phases of gardening, the students strive for credits toward a certificate issued by the National Council after successfully passing five courses, and successfully having competed and won five blue ribbons in "accredited" flower shows. The certificates, issued only to members of the National Council organization, entitle the garden club member to act as a judge in the competitions of the amateur flower show.

ADRIEN BOUTRELLE

A prize-winning arrangement of tulips, anemones, and pussy willows, designed by Mrs. H. Bogart for the pewter class in the Federated Garden Clubs of New York section of the 1954 New York Flower Show.

In the Japanese style Mrs. James McCanne at the California International Flower Show, 1954, combined blade leaves, geranium foliage, and Dutch iris with freesias. This grouping suggests natural growth.

There are now more than 3500 such accredited judges. The level of flower shows is constantly being raised through this study. Many garden clubs and state federations take part in state or national flower shows and in the garden club section of such shows as the International Flower Show in New York, Philadelphia, Boston, Oakland, Los Angeles, Portland, Chicago. In the New York show the Garden Club Federation of New York State, the Men's Garden Clubs of America, and the Garden Club of America have always had important exhibits. This show is the center of exhibition for the Garden Club of America, and their exhibits are both elaborate and fine. In 1954 their exhibit reproduced "The Captain's House" with both inside and outside devoted to showing "Our Garden Heritage." The costs of such exhibits are prodigious. Although partly subsidized by the International Flower Show, the remainder is contributed by members. An estimated minimum cost of $50,000 in a single year is not out of line.

For the shallow confines of a niche in the captain's house of the Garden Club of America at the New York show, Mrs. T. Wylie Kinney and Mrs. Arnold Tschudy used their accessories uncommonly well for a balanced composition, showing charming simplicity in handling delicate garden flowers.

JUNIOR GARDENING   The program to enlist the interest of "juniors"—children of all ages through the public schools—is one of the most flourishing of present garden club activities. Through flower shows staged just for them, through educational exhibits, young people are being taught, not only to garden, to grow vegetables and flowers, but to know about "Conservation of Natural Resources," "Don't Be a Litterbug," "Save the Wild Flowers," "Protect Our Roadsides," and other attitudes of the garden clubs. Often the teachers are sent to "Conservation Workshops," sponsored by the garden clubs at a cost of $20,000, and in Texas at a cost of $10,000. Gardening is carried to juniors in orphanages, and to girls and women in prisons and the Florence Crittenton Homes. Children in polio hospitals receive the program carried on under garden therapy.

GARDEN THERAPY   That gardening is a way to health and well-being is a deep conviction of the garden clubs. The garden therapy program was started in 1944 during the war, in service hospitals, for psychiatric patients. So effective was it that the program has been continued in veterans' hospitals for mental patients. Women trained to work with such illness under the auspices of the hospital staff, and already trained as practical gardeners, carry on a program in greenhouses in winter and in out-of-door gardens in summer. The Garden Club of New Jersey "Green Thumb Corps" gives countless hours to the rehabilitation of these men. As one of them expressed it, "You can't fool a mental patient who has lost his way in the world, but sometimes he can be led to orientation with reality through the miracle of the growing seed, the cycle of growth and flowering. He feels again a part of living. He escapes from his dreams into a world of reality." When a patient, silent for two years, came back through the beauty of a flower, it was a great day for the Green Thumb Corps. Especially in Texas garden therapy has been developed through garden clubs for the blind. Special tools along a wire allow the blind gardener to follow the row to cultivate with a hoe. Plantings have been made in parks of fragrant flowers, with the plant labels in Braille, and records are being made, translating garden books for use of the blind.

Dramatically placed palm spathes and aspidistra leaves cut a bold outline for clivia blossoms in MODERN PAINTING, by Mrs. Frederick W. Lewis at the Federated Garden Clubs of New York's exhibit at the New York show.

ADRIEN BOUTRELLE

Simplicity—plus an 1803 salver from the Earl of Onslow's English collection—made this arrangement by Mrs. Clarence E. Townsend notable. Redbud foliage, anemone blossoms, and cyclamen foliage all go with the pewter.

This elaborate style, in the tradition of the EMPIRE PERIOD, is a difficult one for the show arranger. This example, by Mrs. I. Oppenheimer of the Federated Garden Clubs of New York, was a prize winner.

PHOTOGRAPHS: ADRIAN BOUTRELLE

SEEDS OF PEACE   That the garden clubs could carry through an international project of good will was spectacularly demonstrated by "Seeds of Peace." In the aftermath of World War II the National Council of State Garden Clubs recognized the responsibility of organizations and citizens of the United States to take an active part in fostering peace in the world by helping the people in Europe to help themselves. In the spring of 1948 when seeds were selling in Europe "by the seed," through contributions amounting to $45,000 from garden club members, 17½ tons of vegetable seeds were sent to the needy people of those countries our government was offering to aid by the Marshall Plan. With the co-operation of Church World Service as the distributing agency 780,000 packages of vegetable and flower seeds were distributed. The Burpee Seed Company supplied the seeds at quantity prices and co-operated in packaging them in garden units of thirteen packages each, enough to supply food for a family of five. Messages on the envelopes containing the garden units carried greetings from the gardeners of America in the language of the country to which the seeds were sent. This was the message:

"The people of the United States have great concern for you, and our hearts and minds are seeking ways to help. We are growing food in our own gardens, and we are sending these seeds that you may have fresh vegetables. The names enclosed are those who have given these garden units and they would like to hear from you. They would like to know who you are and how your garden grew. Do not bother to write in English, if you cannot readily do so, for we will gladly have your letter translated here, and we will treasure it as from a friend. May Peace grow with these seeds and bring us all food and friendship."

More than 3000 letters received from grateful families in Belgium, Holland, Luxembourg, France, Austria, Greece, and the American Zone in Germany remain as documentary evidence that "Seeds of Peace" accomplished the intended mission. They supplied needed food and were accepted in the spirit in which they were given.

In relating such vast activity and accomplishments it is possible only to touch the surface of the influences of garden-club activities, which are expanding year after year in more than ten thousand communities in the United States. It is easy to believe those who say they can tell from its looks whether a town has a garden club. And from the phenomenal growth in numbers it is also easy to believe those who predict that in the next ten years a town without a garden club will be unheard of.

If we must find reasons for garden clubs as we have them in America, perhaps we can say they stem from our flair for organization, or because we like to belong to groups with similar purposes and interests, or that we like to know our neighbors and that sharing what we have gives us pleasure. We are not afraid that belonging to groups will mean regimentation and loss of individuality. In fact belonging to garden clubs is a means to extend the influence of our thinking and our freedom for action. In America garden clubs are not "under the patronage of" any branch of government or of any class of patrons. They are expressions of the right to organize for any purpose whatsoever not contrary to the public good and of our determination not to be dependent upon government for civic benefits we can achieve by ourselves.

"More grows in the garden than the gardener sows."

ACKNOWLEDGMENTS

For assistance given in compiling illustrations for this book, the editor and authors wish to make the following grateful acknowledgments:

CHAPTER I–To Henry E. Huntington Library and Art Gallery (page 8), New York Botanical Garden Library and Miss Elizabeth Hall (pages 10 and 12), W. Atlee Burpee Company (page 10), Massachusetts Horticultural Society (page 14).   CHAPTER II–To Mary Alice and John Roche, and to Tet Borsig (page 35), A. Y. Owen (page 57), Don Knight (page 63), Gottscho-Schleisner (page 69), B. J. Allen (page 75).   CHAPTER IV–To Colonial Williamsburg, Inc., and Dietz Press, Inc., Richmond, Virginia.   CHAPTER VI–To Gottscho-Schleisner, and to Thomas Williams and Colonial Williamsburg, Inc. (pages 136, 138 and 139), Max Tatch (pages 154, 164 and 165), Richard Averill Smith (page 163), Ladislaus Cutak (page 170), John Roche (page 171).   CHAPTER IX–To Allianora Rosse for color drawings.   CHAPTER X–To the photographers, garden clubs, state federations of National Council of Garden Clubs, as indicated, and especially to the *National Gardener,* the National Council officers and chairmen, and the Garden Club of America.

INDEX

269